Theory for the World to Come

Forerunners: Ideas First

Short books of thought-in-process scholarship, where intense analysis, questioning, and speculation take the lead

FROM THE UNIVERSITY OF MINNESOTA PRESS

Theory for the World to Come
Speculative Fiction and Apocalyptic Anthropology

Matthew J. Wolf-Meyer

University of Minnesota Press

MINNEAPOLIS

LONDON

Published by the University of Minnesota Press, 2019
111 Third Avenue South, Suite 290
Minneapolis, MN 55401–2520
http://www.upress.umn.edu

The University of Minnesota is an equal-opportunity educator and employer.

Contents

Wyndham's Rule:
Extrapolation, Intensification, Mutation

THERE'S ONE THING that becomes clear reading John Wyndham's apocalyptic novels: the apocalypse is never singular. Catastrophes might devastate a city, maybe a small country. An earthquake, an epidemic might be a catastrophe. But the apocalypse bundles together multiple forces and changes everything irrevocably. In *Day of the Triffids* (1951), it's not enough to have an alien invasion. The meteors that carry alien plant life to Earth also blind everyone who watches them streak through the atmosphere. The aliens land on Earth and find the blinded humans easy prey and wreak havoc on the human population. Only those protected from the alien light retain their vision, and it is up to them to rebuild human society on isolated islands cleared of the alien invaders. In *The Midwich Cuckoos* (2008), it's not enough that the English village of Midwich is trapped under an invisible dome, an impermeable barrier that traps everyone and everything inside of it. The newly born infants in Midwich all resemble each other, preternaturally blond and blue-eyed—and, it seems, capable of telepathy. What could have possibly made such a thing happen? In answering that question, the small village of Midwich—and the world—will never be the same again. Writing in the period after the Second World War, Wyndham captures the ways that a set of unpredictable events overlay already existing conditions to create a situation that changes how society is organized and how people think about the future. Alien invasions don't occur in a social vacuum; they overlay social unpreparedness—captured in the triffid-induced blindness and the Midwich provinciality. It's not just that no one sees the apocalypse coming but that the series of catastrophes that

1

make up an apocalypse is made more potent through this lack of foresight and compounded by provinciality inspired by modern comfort.

Decades before Wyndham, H. G. Wells imagined alien invasions, too: *The War of the Worlds* (2005) features an invasion that has since become paradigm defining. An unsuspecting Earth is invaded by wily Martians, who wield technologies that far outstrip human achievements. All the machines of war that humans have invented barely scratch the Martian war machines, and all seems lost—until the Martians are brought low by Earthly viruses. The Martians, it seems, catch a cold and, before they know it, are all wiped out. Such is the alien invasion story we like to tell, and it comes with variation, like in *Independence Day* (Emmerich 1996) when aliens are brought low by a computer virus, thanks to a little human ingenuity. But *War of the Worlds* and *Independence Day* are also struck through with provincialism. Despite being global invasions, their stories focus almost exclusively on the plights in a very specific location, England and the United States, respectively. We take for granted that events are unfolding similarly elsewhere and that the tiny changes made in one environment will cascade through the whole of the alien fleet. If only we could always be so lucky to be saved through pure accident or a little human ingenuity, and to emerge unscathed or better for the experience. Years later, Ian Edginton and D'Israeli's *Scarlet Traces* (2003) imagines what the aftermath of Wells's invasion was, with the alien technologies used by the imperial powers of the nineteenth century to entrench their hold on the globe in the years after the war. Things change, but they stay the same, reinforcing already-existing social relations. But if Wyndham's rule holds, there's no saving to be had in such simple fashion. The apocalypses that Wyndham imagines are more unsettling. They fundamentally change how society is constituted after they occur: there's no going back to how things were before. Human society might continue to exist alongside the triffids, but only on its isolated islands; life will continue after the cuckoos leave, but always with the possibility of their return. There is the terror of the event itself—the catastrophe that catches us off guard—but then there is the terror of the ongoing apocalypse: who knows what will happen next and what the ramifications will be? What can possibly be done to prepare for the unexpected? Speculative fiction and social theory both ask us to consider these questions, and in finding answers we make new futures possible.

The future is so hard to imagine these days. We know so many things that will happen: the weirding of weather patterns as a result of global warming; the rising of sea levels, which will flood cities and island nations; the acidification of the ocean, leading to mass extinctions of life in the sea and on land; drought, starvation, and famine as a function of changing weather patterns; the growing tensions between the haves and the have-nots, especially as the have-nots are increasingly subject to the worst of changing climate conditions and geographical displacement; the increasing numbers of the have-nots as a result of automation in the workplace and advances in artificial intelligence; growing animosities between nations based on access to needed resources, and complicated by increasing ethnonationalisms. That all seems to be a given, and how exactly it all plays out is impossible to guess. But then imagine some of the other possibilities—holding aside for a moment the possibility of an alien invasion, benign or otherwise: epidemic diseases gaining footholds due to changing climate conditions and spreading globally thanks to faster and more efficient travel technologies; global and local economic recessions—if not total collapses—as a result of corporate and governmental failures to anticipate changing local and global conditions; earthquakes, wildfires, tsunamis, hurricanes, heat waves, all claiming lives and destroying homes, if not whole cities; food chain disruptions due to the extinctions or displacements of species. Then there are things like errant asteroids striking Earth and rogue states unleashing nuclear or biological warfare against unsuspecting populations. And did I mention alien invasions?

Any one of these events would be a catastrophe in its own right; it would disrupt society and its easy operations and assumptions about social order. But taken together—and it seems like more than one of them will happen, and most of them might, all in quick succession—there's an apocalypse looming. It's no wonder, then, that we have a hard time imagining what happens next—any one of these situations might be able to be modeled, but how do we model them all together? How can we possibly imagine how they'll intersect as emerging conditions laid on top of already-existing and slowly mutating social conditions, like racism, international relations, and the profit motives and class antagonisms of global capitalism? Wyndham's rule suggests that we just can't: there's something about the apocalypse and its multiplicity that defies the imagination and any attempt to model it. And even Wyndham falls prey to this: he can imagine the apocalypse and its local iteration, but the world escapes him.

So, here's Wyndham's rule: The apocalypse is never singular; it is always multiple. In its multiplicity, the apocalypse is unimaginable.

What is to be done when the future eludes our capacities for imaginative play and scientific modeling? One possibility is to imagine them one by one, to play with catastrophes and apocalypses in the confines of a novel or film or study. Speculative fiction does this with aplomb, a tradition Wyndham contributed to, if not wholly shaped. Imagine a catastrophe—a natural disaster, a widespread epidemic, a stand-in alien invasion—and model what happens next across society, from individual lives and families, to cities and nations, to the globe. At their most dramatic, everything changes—but usually humans pull through, if only by the skin of their teeth, and maybe in modified form, like Lilith and her brood in Octavia Butler's *Dawn* (1997); at their most modest, catastrophes are recovered from and the social order is restored, albeit in modified form. These attempts to imagine the apocalypse in its singular forms—and to imagine its aftermaths—produce models to think about society and how it might recover from devastating—if not ontology shattering—events. The theory for the world to come lies in these experiments, individual attempts to imagine, to model, to conceive of a future. It also lies in very real experiments with life after catastrophe, from rebuilding communities in the wake of natural disasters, to individual and family attempts to recover from disease, to societies reconstituting themselves in the wake of settler colonialism. These projects don't bring the future into being so much as make plain possible ways forward—and how they build upon the past.

Social theory and speculative fiction are two sides of the same coin. It is not the case that social theory is the sole provenance of academics nor that speculative fiction is that of science fiction writers. Both traditions ask us to imagine worlds that can be described and depicted, and ask us as audiences to imagine the rules that undergird a society and its human and more-than-human relationships. What are the systems of belief of these people (whoever they are), and how do they impact the everyday experience of identity categories like race, ethnicity, disability, gender, sexuality, and class? What are the bases of identity categories—is there even such a thing as race, ethnicity, disability, gender, sexuality, and class in a given society? What is the role of "human nature," and how does it impact people's relationships with each other and their relationships with nonhumans? What are the institutions that shape society and people's everyday lives? Is it capitalism and representative democracy, or some other economic and political organization? Framing these questions should make it clear that the kinds of questions that speculative fiction writers ask also motivate social scientists and other academics interested in social theory. The very questions that anthropologists, sociologists, and psychologists have been pursuing since the nineteenth century have also been motivating speculative fiction writers, from Mary Shelley, Jules Verne, and H. G. Wells, to our contemporaries (Collins 2008). But such speculation and theorization also underlies all description and depiction, even if it is muted and obscured from notice through social convention. Whenever we ask that someone imagine, we ask them to speculate—to theorize with us—the world that we weave through our descriptions. Speculation is a part of life, and theorization is as well (see Shaviro 2015).

Social theory, like speculative fiction, is always situated. It is situated in its time and place, in its historical moment. It is situated in the lives of the people who develop and implement the theory. And it is situated by its critiques, which themselves arise from particular life histories and social situations. Claims to objectivity in social theory—to universal generalization—are just as fraught as they are in objective claims more generally, whether in the hard or social sciences (Behar 1996; Clifford and Marcus 1986; Daston and Galison 2007; Haraway 1997; Hymes 1974; Latour 1987; Shapin and Schaffer 1989). As often as those points have been made since the 1970s—at least—claims to objectivity creep back in. In some cases, they never left, particularly in laboratory sciences. What is often elided in critiques of objectivity, however, are the ways that social situations and personal histories ensure that progress in social theory—in the sense that social theories are developed that capture experiences of the world rather than determine experiences of the world—is short-circuited (Haraway 1997; Lutz 1995). That "legitimate" knowledge is produced largely by scholars trained at universities in the North Atlantic or influenced by knowledge that has developed out of colonial relationships and their influences has profoundly shaped what forms social theory has taken, as well as the categories relied upon to create theoretical knowledge. This has resulted in social theory seeming to be the property of academics, with speculative fiction being the realm of nonacademics. But such an easy division of labor obscures how speculative knowledge in the academy is, how contingent its production has been, and what the influences of individual lives have on what gets thought and how it is articulated. This is evident in how disciplines have formed, how they have spread, and how they have shaped knowledge production.

Consider two very different examples: Anthropology developed in the nineteenth century as the study of Man, the assumption being that humans (and especially men) were distinct among animals, and that they could be studied apart from other animals. How different anthropology would have been if it had developed as a mode of thought in Papua New Guinea, where humans, yams, and pigs all are thought of as persons. Ancestral spirits and inanimate art count too, both of which are roundly dismissed in the North Atlantic through secular claims to rational objectivity (Gell 1998). Anthropology developed when and how it did because of the colonial situations that state powers in the North Atlantic had become invested in, paired with pseudo-Darwinian theories about the development of Man, evolving from a state of savagery through barbarism to civilization, which conveniently mapped onto the globe to explain the apparent development of societies and people toward a state of modernity determined by university cities in the North Atlantic (Trouillot 2003; Wolf 1982). How different anthropology would look if it had been developed in China, where modernity developed quite differently, where theories of rationality had a much longer history, and the conception of the self-determined individual a much shallower one (Rofel 1999).

Or consider how psychiatry would have developed in Japan rather than in Western Europe. For many Japanese people, the site of personhood is the heart; for Western Europeans, it has long been the brain (Lock 2002). In psychiatry in the United States and elsewhere, this has led, over time, to the imputation of aberrant behaviors to problems in the brain. If the site of personhood had been elsewhere, as in the heart, psychiatry may have focused there instead, and its conception of the self would have articulated very differently. Similarly, with the idea of the individual firmly rooted in North Atlantic philosophical, religious, and political traditions, behavior was seen in early psychiatry as rooted in the individual. "Hysterical" women were seen as individual problems, not reactions to patriarchal power structures and social organization that systematically disempowered women from making decisions that they were simultaneously told were the marks of prized, liberal personhood: a double bind if there ever was one (Fanon 2008; Metzl 2003; Rose 1996; Wilson 2004). If psychiatry had developed elsewhere—South Asia or Melanesia, for example—where personhood is seen as a relational process rather than an inherent quality of the individual (Strathern 1992), how psychiatric disorders were defined would be different. They would rely more on an understanding of social dynamics and relations between people rather than organic causes isolated in the brain. What we think of as psychiatry and psychiatric problems are entirely indebted to the social origins of the discipline of psychology; if the discipline had arisen elsewhere and spread from that geographical locus to the rest of the world, it would have made the world in a different way.

Such fantasies of disciplinary alternative histories are important, not just as "what if?" stories but also as a means to denaturalize the latent conception that knowledge produced in any discipline is objective. Knowledge, theory, and models are all subject to the same situational histories that have led to the founding of disciplines, the same personal histories, the same contingencies, and same historical processes. There's nothing inevitable about the creation of anthropology, nor its progress from theoretical paradigm to theoretical paradigm; harder to imagine is that physics or biology might not have arisen as a discipline or that they would have developed in ways other than they have. But an Isaac Newton killed in his crib by scarlet fever or Charles Darwin thrown overboard by a rogue wave, and both physics and biology may have developed quite differently. Gravity and natural selection may have been invented as concepts—eventually—or they may have been obscured by other, more dominant theoretical concerns. That Darwin's theory of natural selection was informed by his social position is well documented (Desmond and Moore 1994); what if he hadn't lived a life of relative privilege, watching those around him, better looking and richer, getting married while he remained a bachelor? What if, instead, he was just a little handsomer and wealthier? He may never had boarded the Beagle, and, even if he had, he might not have conceptualized selection as a struggle or that it was best expressed in reproduction over time. Contingency is critical to the dominance of models and theories that develop, just as much as historical situations ensure that some ways of thinking take precedence over others. A successful theory works on the aggregate—

it relies on making sense to a wide swath of people who employ the theory and use it to shape their interactions with the world. We should be constantly skeptical of the theories that are developed, not only for the motives of their makers but for the ways that they reinforce already-existing conceptions of the world, of persons and institutions, power relations, and particular forms of speculating about the present and the future. That so much of how we think about the world comes from theories developed in the imperial, global North Atlantic should be pause for consideration; there are other ways to think of the world, to build social theory, to speculate about our futures, and to imagine, critically, the failures that North Atlantic traditions have precipitated.

Because of these determinants of social theory, I have a suspicion that the theories that have developed and gained traction over the last half century are deeply suburban. Theory that has been developed since the 1950s has emerged from a North Atlantic sense of comfort, a lack of hardship, an acceptance of global, national, and local power relations, an acceptance of a certain kind of inevitability inspired by a general level of prosperity. In this respect, consider the appeals of J. K. Gibson-Graham's tripartite understanding of capitalist, alternative capitalist, and noncapitalist modes of exchange (Gibson-Graham, Cameron, and Healy 2013). For Gibson-Graham, the model of capitalism they forward captures how there are those exchanges that participate in the capitalist market—buying an industrially produced loaf of bread at the corporate-chain grocery store. And there are alternative forms of exchange, namely purchasing a loaf of bread from a locally owned baker who sources ingredients from family-owned organic farms. Alternative capitalist exchanges help to distribute wealth outside of corporate contexts, supporting laborers more directly without the need to appease corporate shareholders. Finally, there are noncapitalist modes of exchange: I make a loaf of bread from ingredients that I have grown and milled, and I give my loaf of bread to a friend in exchange for his or her labor. Such a conception of alternative capital exchange can exist at a moment in the history of capitalism when institutions that facilitate such forms of exchange are supported, institutions like farmers markets, which are available in some but not nearly all markets. But it is also true that capitalist institutions rely on alternative capitalist formations as the basis for expansions of the market: Whole Foods, a national grocery chain, trades on its appearance as an alternative to corporate chains, when it is just as corporate and dependent on capital as any of the other national chains. Similarly, an understanding that there is an outside of capitalism is a very peculiar fantasy that depends on imagining the existence of property that hasn't been captured by national or private claims to ownership; the seeds to grow wheat have increasingly become proprietary, as are most fuel sources that could conceivably bake a loaf of bread. And yet, Gibson-Graham's conception of capitalism is appealing; it's compelling to imagine that one is participating in some alternative to the hegemony of capital through frequenting a farmers market, even if it is in the microscopic monetary exchanges that support local growers and noncorporate farms. But the success of the theory depends in no small amount on individuals extrapolating from these small exchanges to the entire basis of the economy and its formation.

Or consider the recent turn to multispecies ethnography and animal studies in the social sciences and humanities (Haraway 2003, 2008; Hartigan 2014; Kirksey 2015). That animals had been left out of scholarly consideration for the last century of the university might easily be claimed to be a function of there being more pressing concerns—Civil Rights and the history of racism; gender, sexuality, and feminism; postcolonial politics; globalization and U.S. hegemony; the postmodernist critique of objectivity and knowledge production—and now we are rethinking the category of the human, human agency, and the role of animals in human society. The analytic worm turns, and focus becomes ever narrower in its objects. Anticipating what comes next is beside the point; the challenge is that when scholarly attention continues to work within North Atlantic traditions, drawing on the sources and disciplines that have shaped attention over the last century, the possibility of a rupture, of finding something truly new, is impossible. Instead, new objects are fit into already-existing theoretical matrices, taming the objects as sources of knowledge while reinforcing dominant ways of knowing the world. Take, for example, recent attention to the microbiome, that teeming mass of microbes that covers human bodies and fills our digestive system (Yong 2016): yes, attention to the determinative powers of the microbiome has the potential to reshape how we think about human desires, particularly related to food, but it also tames the microbiome into a knowable object, first in the laboratory and then in the humanities and social sciences. It becomes subject to already-existing ways of knowing, of acting upon it, of conceptualizing it. Its alienness, its unexpected potentials and actions will be translated into models, theories, and language that adhere in disciplines as they already exist. Newness becomes the fetish of disciplinary knowledge production precisely because the new is always impossible to bring into being—because the new is always trapped in disciplinary modes of knowing.

The disciplines are ruled by their comfort and their suburban complacency. And I am no different. Raised in an upper middle class home, in a periurban part of metropolitan Detroit nearly thirty miles from the city center, I attended a private elementary school and an elite public high school. Unlike many of my peers, I opted for a liberal arts education while they attended larger state schools; where most of my peers got by on allowances provided by their parents, I chose to work throughout high school and college, in part to support my game-playing and comic-book-reading hobbies. When college was over, I spent time teaching elementary school, and then migrated into a series of graduate programs. Although there were precarious times, I could always rely on my parents and student loans through the federal government for support. Over time, through work and good fortune, I've found myself gainfully employed, a homeowner, the parent of two children, blissfully free of debt. Maybe you see yourself in that description—

or a version of yourself that you aspire to be or have left behind. Maybe you've been more fortunate than me or made different decisions. But if you're reading this, chances are that we have more in common that we hold in difference. And maybe you too are struck with a kind of suburban comfort, a complacency that seeks, discretely, to reinforce already-existing modes of knowledge production and theoretical models. And maybe, like me, you've become a little dissatisfied with the futures that are being made for us and that are foreclosing the development of other possibilities. Maybe you too want to choose a different future.

Maybe it was that suburban comfort that propelled me into reading all of the speculative fiction that I did throughout my teenage years and into my adulthood. In an era before the internet, I would scour bookstores for Philip K. Dick novels that had long been out of print, and stumbled upon authors like Samuel Delany and Thomas Disch, Joe Haldeman and H. Beam Piper, Ursula Le Guin and Octavia Butler, Norman Spinrad and Cordwainer Smith, by diligently reading the backs of books in search of something else compelling. I had long tired of Isaac Asimov and Robert Heinlein, both of whom seemed too out of touch with reality—a strange criticism for science fiction writers. I wanted fiction that helped me make sense of the world around me but that also unsettled me in productive ways. In essence, I wanted social theory before I knew that there was such a thing to be had, and speculative fiction supplied it. Is it any wonder then that I gravitated toward the discipline of anthropology, a social science that is fundamentally built upon the postapocalypse of global settler colonialism?

Arguing that fiction writers are products of their biographies, their historical situations, and their biases is less controversial than suggesting the claims to objectivity that social scientists implicitly (and sometimes explicitly) make need to be interrogated. Inasmuch as fiction authors are taken to be exemplary thinkers of their time, they are also treated as symptoms—as expressions of cultural trends, some of which might be subtle in their shaping of individuals (Barthes 1977; Foucault 1998). Authors are important not merely for who they are but as one of many, as part of an aggregate that is considered a generation. Reading across the speculative fiction that emerged in the 1960s as a response to the hard science fiction of the immediate afterwar period, a growing concern about the suburban fantasies of the United States becomes clear: from Le Guin's critiques of capitalism in *The Dispossessed* and gender norms in *The Left Hand of Darkness* (1969), to Spinrad's *The Iron Dream* (1972) and its critique of racial fascisms, to Disch's meditations on urbanism and kinship in *334* (1999), to Dick's unease with all the convenience and comfort of the afterwar period, from *Ubik*'s (2012b) talking smart devices to *The Man in the High Castle*'s (2012a) paranoid awareness of something having gone deeply wrong with society to lead to the Nazis and Imperial Japan carving up a defeated United States. In the speculative fiction of the 1960s, there was a palpable dis-ease with suburban comfort—a comfort that was largely predicated on consumerism, patriarchy, and implicit white supremacy. Any social theory that arose from this matrix might rightly be treated with suspicion; any speculative fiction that arose from the same period might serve to put into relief the implicit attempts to normalize suburban hegemony, benefiting from not existing within the university disciplinary system, which implicitly—and sometimes explicitly—sought to diagnose the contemporary moment as a unilineal result of the civilization process. In so doing, social theory operated teleologically, diagnosing the present as an effect of an inevitably unfolding past series of events. But speculation works differently, and drawing from authors whose biographies lent a critical stance to the theories they operated with led them to question the seemingly inevitable. They questioned what would happen if the seemingly inevitable continued in an extrapolative fashion. What would happen if the inevitable intensified, or what if something truly strange and unpredictable happened?

This is all to suggest that social theory is a question of biography, social location, and institutional situation. Social theory and its production is a question of scale—of moving from the lives of individuals, to communities, to society at large, and ever outward spatially. But it is also to suggest—like Frederick Jackson Turner's theory of the frontier (1998)—that social theory also traffics in time. It is also to suggest—somewhat paradoxically—that, like Roland Barthes's discussion of the "death of the author" (1977), biography is less important than social location. This is how a generation can occur, with a shared sensibility across different life experiences. It is also to explain why this book looks the way that it does. My assumption is that you, like me, are a product of a particular moment, and that my dissatisfaction with available theories, with the teleological diagnosis of white supremacy, with the resignation in the face of planetary collapse, is shared. My biography, represented in part in the diary entries that make up the spine of this book, may be my own, but it is not unique; it is singular, but the experiences I have had throughout my life echo in the lives of others. My sensibilities, shaped as they have been by upbringing, education, and my media environment, are the product of the world that I have inherited. My seeking out of alternatives to dominant social theories handed down to me by my disciplines is presumably also shared by others—evident in the growing interest in alternatives to Eurocentric, diagnostic theories. One source for these alternative theories is speculative fiction in its proper sense, but the speculative impulse arises elsewhere, too—in music, in film, in countergenealogies of thought that resurface traditions and thinkers that have been dismissed as not fitting into the dominant body of social theory.

We are at a moment where we need to choose our future. Diagnostic theories will only get us so far. Our imaginations can only get us so far, as well. Both are impoverished by their social locatedness. Accepting both of those claims might inspire resignation. But the purpose of this little foray into the speculative is to inspire the opposite: what sources might there be for rethinking the future? for dislodging the futures that we have been given and to think something anew? for rethinking the past that has gotten us to this point? Articulating futures—imagining them and bringing them into being—is an active process, and rather than a posture of resignation, theory for the world to come needs to instill radical curiosity. That curiosity should be about sources—about texts and authors—as much as it is about practice. The disciplinary configurations that make up the terrain of social theory, embodied in the contemporary neoliberal university, are insufficient at best and harmful at worst. Choose your future: throw in with what has been or try to find something that disrupts the futures we have been given.

There's something appealing about desolation, about the radical reduction of society to its barest elements. Maybe it's the sheer simplicity of it all: agrarian villages in the wake of nuclear holocaust, communitarian solidarity in the aftermath of global economic collapse, transformations in gender roles and sexual mores as a result of alien invasion. Wiping the slate clean makes imagining the future so much more possible. But the future we face won't be based on a clean slate—instead, it will be Wyndham's future, built upon the already-existing blindnesses that adhere in our societies, made possible by our provincialities, our comforts, our prejudices. The future is unfathomable. But in this openness, it becomes a space to play with theories of what might be, of what the future holds, how it will reshape human lives and society, and how the future will change too. Putting theory into the world makes new worlds possible—it creates new lines of flight that human action follows, unfolding in turn new possibilities. Speculative fiction—and social theory—that considers desolation and its aftermaths helps to point to ways forward, ways to live through the apocalypse, even if living through doesn't manage to keep things the same as they were.

How the end is imagined changes over time, and so are the beginnings that the end spawns. As a child, raised during the tail end of the Cold War, the end always seemed to be nuclear. On Saturdays, after a morning's worth of cartoons, one local affiliate would turn to showing horror and science fiction movies—sometimes Japanese *kaiju* movies, starring Godzilla and his nuclear-inspired ilk, sometimes films like *Night of the Comet* (Eberhardt 1984), that fictionalized nuclear holocaust through unexplained phenomena. Looking back, I wonder what sadist programmed these movies to air following Saturday morning cartoons; who in their right mind would think that it was appropriate to show a film featuring flesh-eating zombies after Elmer Fudd chasing Bugs Bunny? But then it strikes me that that question is disingenuous. Future making is about communicability (Briggs and Nichter 2009), about giving from one generation to the next a sense of the future they are to inherit. That's how futures are made—not necessarily through deliberation but through infection.

That I would lie in bed as a child, thinking about nuclear holocaust, imagining that any passing airplane could be a Soviet bomber carrying a nuclear payload to devastate suburban Detroit was entirely the point of showing those films. I'm not sure that I could imagine what would happen next—I couldn't imagine that we would return to some form of agrarianism after nuclear conflagration, since those weren't the stories that made it into film. I'm not sure that I could imagine anything other than the event itself. There was something particularly debilitating about the nuclear future: there wasn't anything to be done about it to avoid it, nor was there any recovering from it. The movies I watched on TV—sometimes through a screen of fingers to block out the gore—stopped short of imaging what happened *next*. How, exactly, did human society rebuild itself? What, precisely, did people do to ensure that another nuclear holocaust didn't happen? In effect, not imagining these possibilities ensured that viewers like me never learned a language to elaborate postapocalyptic possibilities.

Utopias are usually boring, even when they're stories of crawling from the wreckage of the apocalypse. And that's what so much of postapoaclyptic literature attempts to skirt around: what's so compelling about societies rebuilding themselves, or, worse yet, societies that have already rebuilt? There must be some threat to the easy life of utopia to make it worth putting into narrative. In a nutshell, that's the motivation for so many of the apocalyptic stories I grew up with, albeit their utopia was the casual, comfortable utopia of 1980s American consumer capitalism. That American utopia was a partial one—it overwhelmingly favored decently educated, suburban white people, who were either in professions protected from recessions or from the globalization of industrial labor; rural and urban communities, each in their own ways, were more exposed to the vagaries of internationalizing and financializing capitalism. But for those in their suburban idylls, utopia was at hand. Not in some ideal sense—it wasn't a suburban heaven— but all needs were met, and wealth accrued. Life wasn't perfect, but it was secure to the extent that it was unlikely that nuclear bombs would actually be dropped.

That utopia was easy to disrupt, and films like George Romero's *Dawn of the Dead* (1978) sought to do just that. Set in a suburban shopping mall, the protagonists take refuge from a zombie infestation that has seemingly infected the rest of the world—or at least the immediate surroundings. Part too-obvious allegory for the blindnesses of consumer capitalism, part postapocalyptic anxiety fantasy, *Dawn of the Dead* doesn't have anything to say about how to rebuild society, how to make good use of the clean slate that the zombies would provide once they were eradicated. That world would wait until *Survival of the Dead* (2009) in which an island-bound community has found refuge from the ever-present zombies—until the zombies begin to make their way to the island under water. But the world of *Survival* is a sadly capitalist one, where the wealthy live in glass towers and think themselves immune from the recurrent waves of the zombie apocalypse. They find themselves unprepared for the teeming masses of zombies that find their way ashore. If Romero has an abiding rule, it is that wealth won't protect you from catastrophe. If anything, wealth tends to make you especially blind to the world through its suburban provincialisms. Rebuilding the world and its consumerist vagaries won't stop the next catastrophe—and the blindness that would seem to justify such rebuilding points to the problems that make our present catastrophes so devastating. There's no way forward, and the route society is on is sure to make the next catastrophe more devastating for lack of planning.

Those apocalyptic Saturday films seemed to suggest that my forebears were resigned to the future that was coming to meet us. Resignation is a powerful force, and one that is infectious: living resignedly tends to infect those who are exposed to it. Resigned imaginations and catastrophic speculations tend to materialize their worlds through inaction—or, rather, actions that are too modest to affect a different future. Resignation makes sense of modest action, of being comfortable, of being maybe a little outraged, but not outraged enough to make a difference. That suburban complacency, that late capitalist utopia that favors some people and their lifestyles over others, is easily fostered through modest action, through a lack of imagination about what comes next. How do we see past our resignations? How do we begin to think past the looming apocalypse, one that will comprise the known and unknown? How do we begin to build a set of theories for the world to come that works past our blindnesses, our complacencies and resignations? How do we design a society that at once is prepared for the array of catastrophes that are on the horizon and will rebound into something new and unprecedented on the other side of the apocalyptic events?

In this book, I begin to think about the theories for the world to come—what theories there are that will help to build a sustainable, equitable world after collapse. Or, maybe, sets of theories that when put into play in the present will change the possible futures that have come to grip our imaginations. Can social theories, mined from specific local spaces and historical moments, inspire new lines of flight, new paths into the horizon that is the future? To answer these questions, I turn to a set of speculative texts—films, novels, television shows, comic books—to consider their embedded social theories: what are the worlds they build, how are they composed, and what kinds of lives do they enable? I think through these texts based on my own history, my own locations and fixations. I consider, in turn, my time in Michigan, in California, and in New York, and the texts that infected me in each of those personal moments. Those texts are largely local themselves, texts produced by or situated in Michigan, California, and New York. The chapters are autobiographic reflections and textual analyses, all in the service of thinking through speculations in their moment and their lingering effects. Throughout, I am interested in three forms of future historiography: intensification, extrapolation, and mutation, each of which helps to expose the problems we currently face in thinking about the future and its possibilities.

Not solely the provenance of speculative fiction, intensification, extrapolation, and mutation are also at the heart of many social theories. Extrapolation takes a force or institution or person and puts it into the future, relatively unchanged. Extrapolating in this way is a means to imagine what will happen to something as it is carried into the future: What will the future of capitalism be? Or the future of kinship relationships? Extrapolation allows for imagining how something like capitalism will respond to other changes, social and environmental. In doing so, extrapolation serves to make evident how fragile or resilient institutions, forces, and people are. Intensification imagines what will happen with the increase in quality of a force or the pervasiveness of an institution. This is not to imagine an institution or force unchanged, but to purposefully toy with making a force unrelenting or an institution more total. What if the world just keeps heating up? What if capitalism becomes so totalizing that all social interactions are subject to the market? Answering these questions is a foray into speculating about intensification. Mutation modulates forces and institutions in unpredictable ways. What if marriage was replaced by the corporation, allowing for more than two people to be married in a joint venture? Or what if the Ice Age suddenly began, despite all our preparations for global warming? Mutation is about surprise, about the unexpected, and how individuals and societies respond.

Each of these modes of thought, which might otherwise be sufficient for predicting the future, run up against Wyndham's Rule: they cannot capture the multifarious forces that conspire to make our collective future. In the following, I turn from the question of life at the end of capitalism to the nihilism of deep time, to the social need for revolution and its relationship to conceptions of time. If intensification, extrapolation, and mutation are insufficient, might the disavowal of power, a graceful handing over of power to the generations in our wake, help to usher in a new set of theories for the world to come?

Detroit Diaries, 1992–1999

I AM OF THE GENERATION of suburban white kids who made forays into Detroit after the mass migration of white families out to the suburbs in the 1960 and 1970s. I grew up first in a second-ring suburb of Detroit, and, at age six, was moved to what would eventually become a distant suburb of the city but, at the time, was basically farm country. My younger brother and I grew up on ten acres of land, near no other small children, bordered by cornfields on one side and a county park on the other. My father continued to practice medicine in the second-ring suburb we started in, commuting back and forth each day, and, at times, working shifts at hospitals in the city proper. The only times I can remember going into the city as a child were to attend sporting events, hockey and wrestling, mostly. It wasn't until I was a teenager, able to drive myself, that I started going to all-ages concerts at the State Theater and St. Andrew's. And then, during my college years, branching out into indie rock shows at the Majestic and Zoot's (a name I am honestly shocked that I remember), and all-night, clandestine raves. Detroit had largely been abandoned by white suburbanites of my parents' generation, although they still trekked into the city for cultural events—the symphony, the opera, sports. By the time my friends and I were venturing into the city, it felt not so much rebellious as exploratory: what had our parents been keeping from us? And why was racism the tool being used to ensure that we didn't go into the city? Or, if we did, that our adventures were targeted and well protected by an ambient and obvious police presence?

I remember sitting on the floor of St. Andrew's on a school night, waiting, interminably, for a band to take the stage, all the while trying to figure out how I would get through the next school day on so little sleep.

I remember sitting on the floor of a bar that had been used that night for a rave, there because police had raided the rave. All white cops and a mixed-race group of party goers. Looking back now, it's clear that so much of the police crackdown on the rave scene was racially motivated—an attempt to keep white kids out of the city, to protect them and to uphold their parents' sentiments about the city.

I remember driving home along Woodward Avenue, the great artery of an earlier era, then largely abandoned, stopping at each red light, followed closely by two men in a truck. When I stopped at yet another red light—at 2:30 AM, when the streets were totally empty except for my car and this other truck—they pulled alongside and motioned down my window. "Why," the driver asked, "was I stopping for all these red lights? It's Detroit!" As they pulled away, I watched them run a series of red lights, disappearing into the urban horizon before me. I still stopped at the lights—and continued to in future trips into the city—but the promise of lawlessness stuck with me. Does it matter that the two men in that truck were black?

My forays into the city—and those of my peers—stood in opposition to the often overt racism of our parents' generation. One of my uncles, an appliance repairman, would often narrate stories of having to take calls in the city and painted a grim picture of people's living situations—garbage-strewn houses, ill-kempt children, near-feral dogs tied up in yards. Another uncle narrated the riots in the city in 1967, when he was serving as part of the National Guard, casting the city as a site of constant racial unrest. Other friends' parents would narrate tales of armed robberies, drug dealers, carjackings, and gang activity. They would also tell the tales of families moving from the city—or first- and second-ring suburbs—to deeper, safer homes in the suburbs. Combined, the stories painted the city as a barren, lawless, postapocalyptic landscape, populated by people who had been left behind. But whom they had been left behind by and what constituted the apocalypse they faced was always unclear.

It was only during my college years, largely through my classes, that I began to piece that history together. Central here was a class that I took on "Detroit," a course offered by three faculty— all white men, all middle aged or older, none of whom grew up in the city or even in the area, as far as I can recall. We read books on Henry Ford and the invention of the automobile and early twentieth-century Detroit (Lacey 1986); books on Father Coughlin and his racist politics (Warren 1996); Coleman Young's autobiography, *Hard Stuff* (Young and Wheeler 1994), notable for being the first black mayor of the city—and a man who endorsed a form of afrocentric politics in a major U.S. city that rejected the white suburbs and their interference; Elmore Leonard novels, like *Unknown Man #89* (1977), which portrayed the suburb where I grew up—Rochester—decades before we moved there. The history of Detroit came in pieces, organized around "great" men, each of whom rallied a moment into being: early industrialization through Ford, antebellum racism through Father Coughlin, post–white flight rejection through Young. And then there were people like Leonard who could play in the worlds that these men had created. Leonard's world is one of lawlessness, the frontier in the city, a meditation on how the small stakes of crime motivate venal action. Leonard reinforced a view of the city as on the verge of dissolution, rife with seedy criminals of all stripes. But it was a visit to the Diego Rivera mural in the Detroit Institute of Art as a class, whereupon one of my professors proclaimed it the "spiritual center of America," that really impressed me; thinking about Rivera's mural as religious captured the totalizing aspect of the art, its attempt to bring the world together, iconographically and relationally, into a map of connections, histories, and forces.

Detroit was built as the Paris of the Midwest, a cultural and spiritual center of the United States, at a time when automobiles were just beginning to make an impact on how cities could be organized. In its earliest urban iteration, Detroit borrowed from

Paris the design of a wheel with a series of spokes radiating out from its center. These spokes—Woodward, Gratiot, Grand River—laid on top of a modernist grid, cutting the city up horizontally and vertically. Maybe on horseback or in a carriage this kind of infrastructure would make sense, but with modern automobiles, it made for a city that was less efficient for being ruled by 6-corner stops. Maybe, in retrospect, that's why my fellow city drivers were so keen to blow through red lights; otherwise, the feeling of waiting pointlessly through minutes of empty green lights feels like too much. The grid radiates out from the Detroit River and city center, with each mile marker named for its distance from the river from 8 Mile onward. Such a naming convention has the benefit of being able to measure one's distance from the city, but, in the racial order of Detroit and its suburbs, it also served as a marker of how far one's white flight carried them. My earliest years were spent at 16 Mile Road, and then we moved near 28 Mile Road. It also, during the period of Detroit's growing gentrification in the 2000s, could be taken as a marker for one's participation in the reverse racialization of the city.

Do what you will with this, then: my first professional job was as an assistant professor at Wayne State University, the city university of Detroit and the only urban university in the Michigan system. It was an unexpected and rather sudden move, taking me from Chicago, where I was living while finishing my dissertation, back to my native Michigan. I tried, unsuccessfully, for two weeks to find an apartment in the city proper, and, when I couldn't, I ended up renting a place in Ferndale, two blocks north of 8 Mile. Ferndale felt like the promise of Detroit to me: quietly integrated, middle class, unpretentious. Being where I was gave me the opportunity to commute home adventurously. From my office off Cass Avenue (sometimes referred to as Cass Corridor), I could take the Lodge Freeway, Woodward, or one of the secondary streets that wound northward. I cut through neighborhoods—Boston-Edison, University Village, Sherwood Forest—to see what they had become during decade or more since I had last driven them.

There were still dilapidated houses, empty mansions, and vacant businesses. I looked at the possibility of buying a home in the city, and joked with my partner about buying an enormous home for pennies on the dollar. Homes that had been a sign of status and prestige in the early twentieth century were reduced to having their unused rooms walled off in order to reduce the cost to heat them, effectively making thirty-room mansions into modest single-family homes. My drive home was often lonely, with mine being the only car on the road—even during rush hour. Yes, parts of the city had become depopulated, in part driven by the lack of local resources, like grocery stores, but other parts of the city were alive with communities that had been obscured by the racism of my parents' generation. As I got to know my coworkers, some of whom lived in the city proper and had called it home for generations, I slowly started to see the city differently. I started to see how the gentrification efforts were displacing more organic, sometimes longstanding, partnerships between already existing community members (Hartigan 1999). I started to see beyond the edifices of the city that I had relied on—sites like John King's enormous used bookstore, Mexican Village, the Eastern Market—and started to see the jazz and blues clubs, the community art projects, the local restaurants. Detroit started to feel like three cities: the city of fear fostered by an older generation, the city of exploration I forayed into, and the city that was actually there. That last city was different than I imagined it to be, but I had been blinded to it by generations before me, the media that cast Detroit as a city of fear, and my own habits. Detroit had become a palimpsest, three cities (maybe more), laid atop one another, each with its own history, its own present, and its own possible futures. Each of those futures, however, was struck through with the politics of race, a politics that ensured that, however the future developed, it would be as an effect of racial histories and presents that Detroiters and their suburban brethren had become entrenched in over the preceding century or longer, and that had intensified since the 1960s.

The shadow of the city was always its suburbs, a shadow built on the segregation of white and black populations. For suburban, white communities, Detroit was a postapocalyptic scene—a city crawling from the wreckage of industrial abandonment, a fleeing white population (which took a lot of wealth with it), the riots themselves, and the ongoing dismissal of white expertise on the part of Detroit's black leadership. What was the original catastrophe, and how did it turn into the urban apocalypse that resulted? Based on my parents' generation's telling, it was the race riots in 1967. What they elided were the decades of redlining, the destruction of communities through the development of highways that cut through black neighborhoods; the consolidation of labor power in the hands of whites; the racism—implicit and explicit—of employers like Henry Ford; the segregation of schools, workplaces, and neighborhoods (Sugrue 1998). None of this was unique to Detroit—it happened throughout U.S. cities in the period after the Second World War and before the Civil Rights movement (and after Civil Rights, too). But Detroit was at the forefront in a particularly technological way: the automobiles that made Detroit possible facilitated the construction of necessary expansions of the highway system to support the transportation of goods, the demands for automobiles, and the growing communities of commuters who were traveling ever-longer distances into the city. The automobile and its concrete environment—and the desires of Americans to drive—enabled lawmakers and city planners to make particular kinds of decisions about how to build that environment, which advantaged some at the expense of others. Underlying these drives were the impulses of Fordist capitalism, which pushed consumption into new directions that built on old expectations, particularly of individuality and self-determination. The originary catastrophe was the two-edged sword of automobility, which at once made speedy transportation possible, revolutionizing the economy, but which simultaneously made once-compressed communities into sprawling, suburban nightmares (Lutz and Lutz Fernandez 2010).

The suburbs are their own particular form of hell. It's hard to imagine that when settlers first came to North America they could imagine what urban planning, racial tensions, and automobility would do to the continent. Throughout my college years, I took advantage of the infrastructural developments of the Eisenhower era, taking road trips from Michigan westward, southward, and eastward. Between my early twenties and my late thirties, I counted eleven trips between Michigan and California, all by car. Over the years, I took innumerable flights across the United States, gazing downward at the concrete arteries that cut across the continent and comprise the nervous systems of city-suburban-rural sprawl. Is it any wonder, then, that I became fixed on Paolo Soleri's utopian urban solution Arcosanti (Soleri 1970)? Arcosanti—and Soleri's proposed arcologies—takes the American impulse to build ever outward, to find a plot of land for each family, to extend into every inch of what was once the frontier, but is now just property to be passed from person to person through financial exchange, and inverts the sprawl of the suburbs into a massive building that goes upward instead out outward. As the continent gets carved into property, town squares became downtowns, which turned into suburban shopping malls, and eventually strip malls—repetitions of the same fast-food restaurants, corporate pharmacies, clothing and other sundry stores, all in the name of convenience. Now, decades after the invention of the shopping mall and the expansion of the strip mall, vacant downtown properties offer a space for gentrification and the revitalization of city centers, and Amazon's proposed drones promise to do to shopping malls and strip malls what malls did to city centers. The sprawl of my youth—Kmart, Barnes & Noble, Taco Bell, McDonald's, JoAnn Fabrics—is slowly being displaced in favor of empty, anonymous retail space, concrete slabs and empty carcasses of convenience. Throughout my teenage and young adult years, the suburban blight of convenience made up a world that I constantly imagined rebelling against—and yet, the numbing effects of convenience made any open rebellion impossible to consider. Instead, the forms of rebellion that were made possible were intensely personal, and led me—and others of my generation—to adventure into the city that our forebears had largely rejected. And, for some, it led to their investments in gentrification: making Detroit white again, or at least whiter than it had been for two generations.

The evacuation and abandonment that white people did to the city, captured perfectly in what happened to Detroit over the last century, will now be done to them, by themselves. The logic of convenience will undo the suburbs in the same way that it undid the city, with the same erosion of community and social connections, but this time, with the distances between homes, the divestment from public infrastructure like education and health care, there will be no easy solutions, and the potential for real catastrophes magnifies as a result. Robert Kirkman's zombie postapocalypse *The Walking Dead* captures this well: in the face of swaths of the population turning into flesh-eating zombies, there is seemingly no resistance, no concerted effort to stop the zombie infection—a solution easy to imagine in any tightly knit community. Instead, society just crumbles in the face of people turning into the undead. That's all fine, and par for the course in zombie narratives. But what begins to happen much later is a series of attempts to create and sustain an interconnected set of settlements of survivors (Kirkman and Adlard 2015). Each of the settlements has been carved into being by dedicated work on the part of a group of idealists, although some favor authoritarian rule over more benign democratic anarchy. As the settlements begin to connect into a loose trade federation, they come into conflict with despotic villains interested in enslaving the more peaceful communities for their own benefit. Kirkman's zombie postapocalypse captures the downstream effects of American suburban blindness and selfishness: people can't think proactively, they can't make a real plan for the future, and they surely can't make a plan that contributes to their collaborative development of a post–zombie infection society, whatever it might look like. The survivors—most of whom are white, seemingly former suburbanites—are doing it to themselves with in-fighting, but, more importantly, a sheer lack of vision. They can't seem to imagine what the future could be, with or without zombies; they did it to themselves, after all, since whatever brought on the disaster was something, presumably, made or facilitated by those in power. White people.

White Futures and Visceral Presents: *Robocop* and P-Funk

PAUL VERHOEVEN'S *ROBOCOP* (1987) starts with a news program featuring a story on the city-state of Praetoria, once of South Africa but now independent after some political upheaval, announcing that they have a French-supplied neutron bomb and are ready to use it. This marks the one and only mention of race in the film, a story set in a futuristic Detroit, which at the time the film was made was led by a black mayor, Coleman Young, and had a predominantly black population—nearly two-thirds of the citizens of Detroit were black, with another third being mostly white. But it's clear, in Verhoeven's placement of that short news item, that race continues to be a source of tension in *Robocop*'s future society; in Detroit, however, it seems like white flight has reversed course entirely, and outside of a black middle manager in the nefarious Omni Consumer Products (OCP) and a black henchman of the criminal mastermind, Clarence, there are only extras to disrupt the monotonous whiteness of the film. Watching it now, it's hard to imagine what could have happened between 1986 and 2043—when the film is set—that could so totally upend the racial mixture of the city, especially when one of the critical plot points in the story is that Old Detroit is so crime ridden that it calls for robot police to eradicate crime there in order for Delta City to be developed—so that two million workers can flood into the city. The Old Man, which is how the head of OCP is referred to throughout the film, reflects on his boyhood spent in Old Detroit, and how it has fallen into the hands of criminals; in the script, Alex Murphy, who will later be the titular Robocop, also recalls a childhood spent in Old Detroit. Something, it seems, happened a long time ago that led to reverse migration into the city from the suburbs. Or, it was simply lazy filmmaking, substituting Dallas of 1986 for Detroit of 2043, and ignoring the racial realities of Detroit at the time. Or the story of Detroit—and the Detroit that is being played out in this story of robotics and automation—is a story about whiteness and the control of the future.

Our hero, Murphy, is a good cop. The viewer knows this not through any robust backstory but through the actor Peter Weller's easy smile and admission that his gun-handling tricks are indebted to his attempt to impress his son and modeled on the TV hero T. J. Lazer. He jokes with his female partner, Lewis, and rushes into action, eager to uphold the law. When this eagerness leads him into Clarence's headquarters, he gets the drop on two henchmen but is then overwhelmed by Clarence and the rest of his crew. They tease him until they begin to torture him, first shooting off his right hand, his right arm, wounding both legs and torso, and eventually Clarence apparently kills him with a shot to the head, which throws chunks of skull and brain into the air, just to make it clear how damaged Murphy has become. A manager at OCP has been waiting for just such an event, and his team works to turn Murphy into Robocop, replacing his body with a titanium exoskeleton, but saving Murphy's brain and face, which is largely concealed under his visor. Robocop's development depended upon the failure of ED-209, a fully automated policing robot developed by a more senior manager at OCP. During a demonstration, ED-209 malfunctions and kills a middle manager who is playacting the role of a criminal, threatening ED-209 with a gun. The lesson is plain: full automation is dangerous, but an android—a robot with the sensibilities of a human—is exactly what the city needs. And this android, Robocop, has the soul of a white man who can recall a time when Detroit wasn't the crime-ridden dump it has become, waiting to be gentrified into Delta City.

Thinking about *Robocop* in its moment—a moment when Japanese automotive manufacturing was making significant inroads into the American market, and in which the Big Three (Ford,

General Motors, and Chevrolet) were going through financial hardship and restructuring—*Robocop* brings into relief the fears of a future of automation and of corporate control of everyday life. *Robocop*'s future is a jaundiced one, where the tendencies of its moment are extrapolated into intensified versions of themselves. Meanwhile, so much remains the same: clothing, cars, homes and furniture, guns and uniforms. Everything is so familiar, except for the lumbering cyborg protecting the city. There's nothing alien about this future; for some, it might even be a comforting future, a Detroit returned to its original whiteness, a city tamed by the still-somewhat-human Robocop. A machine haunted by the memories he has of a wife and son, of their suburban home, fighting against corporate interests—and the full automation of American labor. Whatever the catastrophes occurring in the real world, whatever the fears people may have about the racial makeup of the city, of economic neoliberalization, of crime, *Robocop* suggests that the future won't be foreign.

The filming script cuts a significant subplot from the previous versions of the script that centers on the police voting to strike due to the appalling work conditions under which OCP forces them to work. In previous scripts, the neoliberalization of the police force leads to this strike at a critical moment in the story, with the police walking off the job just as ED-209's backer, Dick Jones, is revealed to have been in cahoots with Clarence all along. Clarence's gang leads a riot in the city, unchecked by the lack of police. Given military-grade weapons and a tracking device by their corporate benefactor, Clarence and his gang follow Robocop to an abandoned mill, where they ambush him and Lewis. With no police backup, and the city wracked by riots, Robocop and Lewis must fend for themselves against Clarence's rogues. Robocop and Lewis survive, leading to Robocop's final confrontation with Dick Jones, the corporate raider behind ED-209. Jones's duplicity is revealed during a final board meeting, leading both to his dismissal by the Old Man and execution by Robocop. But the strike is precisely where *Robocop 2* (Kershner 1990) picks up the story, with the city of Detroit in default to OCP for the money owed for their management of the city's police, and OCP threatening foreclosure on the city. The goal for OCP is revealed to be the neoliberal corporate fantasy of replacing the city government with OCP's capitalist bureaucracy. The central drama is whether Robocop is actually human or entirely a machine masked as human, a drama played out against the backdrop of the expansion of a new drug, Nuke, into the market. The white future of Detroit is one ruled by corporations, controlled by robotic, automated police, and sedated by white drug dealers. "Make 'Made in America' mean something again!" the Old Man intones while announcing the corporate takeover of the city, and what it seems to mean is that the paternalistic corporation will achieve its apotheosis in the displacement of politics in favor of shareholder appeasement.

OCP promises us that "the future has a silver lining," thanks to its development of Delta City. But that future is ruled by corporations, where whites have resumed control of the city. It is a future that dresses up the present in a technophilic costume of titanium and heavy weapons. Its thrills are visceral ultraviolence, all flesh subsumed by metal, armor, and corporate greed. Maybe in the 1980s it seemed simultaneously like the future had already arrived and no other future would ever come. Maybe that's why Ford Probes, which seemed so futuristic at the time, filled the futuristic police fleet, and how Dallas could substitute for a future Detroit. How irrepressibly white.

And then there was the strange afrofuturism of George Clinton, captured in the spacey tropes of the Mothership, including raunchy lyrics about sex and psychedelic drug use. If Verhoeven's *Robocop* offers a dour future inextricable from the racialized present built upon the visual fascination of a robotic man and his justified killings (Shaviro 1993), Clinton's afrofuturism relies on entendre, suggestion, and continuity-building referentiality to build an intensified world of visceral connection (Weheliye 2014; Womack 2013; Youngquist 2016). Stretching between the late 1960s and the middle 1980s, Parliament and Funkadelic released albums annually, toured consistently, and established themselves as a politically and musically progressive voice in contemporary American music. What they didn't do, however, was synthesize their various fictional, political, and music statements into a coherent manifesto.

"Funk," for Clinton and his collaborators, was a feeling, a rhythm. Funk is an alternative viscerality. Popular music of the era—disco, mainstream rock and roll, the growing underground punk and heavy metal scenes, the lingering progressive rock trend—could be reduced to music that was largely anesthetic in its effects, or, if it produced feeling, they were feelings that accorded with normative expectations. Heavy metal and punk offered violence and discontent distilled into black-clad faux nihilism; disco offered a sexuality fueled by heteronormative gender roles, which Clinton referred to as "the blahs" and "like fucking with one stroke." Funk offered a form of embodied experience that struck out at these white, dominant forms of musical aesthetics. After decades of white appropriation of black musical forms, P-Funk offered a distilled critique of the go-nowhere complacency that popular music had become. If not a revolution in politics, P-Funk offered a visceral experience that was characterized by a focus on the body and its repressed features, foremost among them bodily waste and sex. Funk takes on the properties of a substance, a viscous, corporeal groove that binds people together in a psychedelic experience. But, rather than the psychedelia of Timothy Leary and the 1960s, which focuses on "tuning in" to hallucinatory experiences, the psychedelia of P-Funk is rooted in bodily experience, in a connection to the Earth that is evident in our most material of bodily experiences. There's no "dropping out" for Clinton, only "turn[ing] you on," in contrast to Robocop's anesthetized corporeality.

If there is anything close to a manifesto in the work of P-Funk, it is "Standing on the Verge of Getting It On," a song from their 1974 album of the same name. In it, Clinton sings, "You really shouldn't ought to fight it / The music is designed to do no harm / It's just for you / With just a little bit of effort / I can and well, we might just turn you on / Even if you don't admit it / The time for change is here and here we are / We're just for you." Clinton's lyrics are rife with double entendre so blatant they lack subtext entirely; here, "getting it on" is both a reference to sexual intercourse and experiencing the libidinal energies of funk itself. But those lyrics follow an interchange that gets at the heart of Clinton's libidinal conception of life: "Hey lady won't you be my dog and I'll be your tree / And you can pee on me," he entreats his listener, and it's immediately clear that this is no suburban love song. There's no subtle romance, no polite seduction to be had; instead, there's just the crass sexuality of "dogs" and "bitches." If Clinton's lyrics are unsettling, it's precisely because they traffic in a carnal conception of sexuality, one freed from the polite Protestantism of American nuclear families—and one that seems to treat men and women as equal in their desiring capacities. If it's a turnoff, you might be taking it too seriously. Or, at least, you might be thinking about it too much: funk, at its best, is a feeling, a groove, a way of experiencing your body, a way of being connected to the world in the present. Appeals to carnality attempt to root listeners in the present, in the joking mood of playacting a tree and dog, in disrupting the suburban niceties of dinner and a movie. P-Funk's viscerality seeks to break through the present, the calm of a Fleetwood Mac song on the radio, providing something else, a contrary way to conceptualize one's embodied present and relations with other people and the world. Hallucinogens aren't going to help you get it on, but a little bit of estrangement brought about through the Motherhship might.

If "Standing on the Verge of Getting It On" offers a foray into the sexual politics of P-Funk, "Promentalshitbackwashpsychosis Enema Squad (the Doo Doo Chasers)" is a clear statement of Clinton's scatological appeal. Combining a critique of American political life and the kind of subjects it produces, Clinton simultaneously offers one of his most trenchant lyrics about the state of the American consumer and the appeal of the corpological. "The world is a toll-free toilet," Clinton sings, "Our mouths neurological assholes / And psychologically speaking / We're in a state of mental diarrhea / Talking shit a mile a minute / Or in a state of constipated notions / Can't think of nothin' but shit / And in this world of / Stinky futures, shitty memories and / Constipated 19 now-nows / Emerges from the hiney of your head / The doo doo chasers." Those "constipated 19 now-nows"—in Clinton's case, the late 1970s—seem to be going nowhere, in no small part because "we're in a state of mental diarrhea." Elsewhere on the album, he sings about his inability to "get into the neutron bomb" and a litany of other modern threats. The modern world is full of "drug addict principle[s]," things "that would close the door," "poisoned land," and "bad romance," resulting in our "constipated notions." It's this view of the present, of the failures of imagination, of feeling, that Clinton seeks to remedy, that funk serves as a palliative for. A decade later, *Robocop* seems to confirm everything that Clinton was critiquing: a white, machinic human, trying to reclaim a city from "crime," totally desensitized to his body, deprived of all desire, and fed by something that "tastes like babyfood." But Robocop never seems to shit; he really is a "constipated notion," a future that is radically out of touch with his humanity.

It isn't so much that Clinton and his P-Funk collaborators offer an afrocentric future as they do a countergenealogy of the present, one in which the visceral, the corporeal, takes precedence over the cognitive. The Mothership is not from the future so much as it offers an alternative present, one in which the libidinal experiments of Dr. Funkenstein are properly liberating, freeing one's "mind" so one's "ass can follow." The Mothership and its mission are the return of the repressed, doubly so: the body and its vulgar capacities are resurfaced for their anticivilizational effects, and dominated black artists, subject to the hegemonic effects of American popular culture, articulate a visceral mode that rejects the hermetic faux escapism and channeled suppression of contemporary music. P-Funk had a solid run from the late 1960s through the early 1980s, ending during a period in which Clinton was consumed with legal battles to reassert his ownership of the rights to the music that he had recorded. But, simultaneously, P-Funk seems to have run out of momentum. By his own account, Clinton was hooked on crack cocaine (Clinton and Greenman 2014), many of the participating musicians had become involved in other musical projects, and popular music was moving toward rap and hair metal. The Reagan 1980s seemed like the wrong place for P-Funk to inhabit, and the Mothership's mission was officially over. *Robocop* and its impoverished, retread future was the kind of future that Americans had become invested in; the visceral present that P-Funk offered seemed to be out of place, if not totally alien. Better, it seems, to invest in the hyperviolent reclamation politics of *Robocop,* an empty vessel for the white revanchist politics of the gentrifying city.

If *Robocop* offers a future of whiteness—mechanized, featureless, haunted by a past that is impossible to reclaim, bodies that eat but do not shit—then P-Funk offers its opposite. It doesn't feel entirely accidental to me that *Robocop* is set in Detroit and that Clinton found a home there for years, first working for Motown as a songwriter, and then working on several P-Funk albums there. Detroit was a city of tomorrow, first in the early part of the twentieth century when it forecast a world of endless roads and manufacturing jobs for the working class, and then, after white flight, it offered a vision of minority rule—what Clinton referred to as "Chocolate City" on a Parliament album of the same name. Maybe in another era—one in which the manufacturing base was intact—a minority-led city could have been successful, but Detroit faltered in no small part due to antagonisms between municipal leaders in the suburbs and the city. I was too young to know any of what was happening in the city. The cleverness of Southeast Michigan's urban planning is such that one can drive into the city from any direction and be visually unaware of what is happening at street level: the highways largely exist below street level with tall soundproofing walls protecting neighborhoods from traffic noise, but also obscuring the vision of suburban drivers commuting into the city. One can leave home and arrive in the downtown stadium and theater district and never see a Detroit neighborhood, never coming into contact with the everyday realities of life in the city. In that void of civic experience, it's easy to imagine a city rife with crime, like *Robocop* does.

Clinton didn't do much to appeal to white listeners, and as the 1980s wore on and he returned to making music, he was less invested in funk and more directed at emerging "urban" radio, which built on his deepening reputation among hip hop artists as a father of afrofuturism. Meanwhile, *Robocop* would inspire two sequels, with diminishing returns; whereas the first film was cluelessly out of touch with the urban realities of Detroit and struggled with the inevitabilities of industrial automation, the later films pit *Robocop* against white drug dealers and had him team up with a band of mostly white people in an attempt to resist the corporate gentrification of the city (Dekker 1993). Whatever visceral thrills might have underwritten the first film, with its hyperviolence and car chases, its absurd critique of corporate America, and its sentimental robot, by the time the films had become a serial, Robocop was merely a vessel for vapid critiques of American corporatism. Like Robocop himself, the films became empty of any humanity; the politics they forwarded were insubstantial too, defanged of any proper critique, any vision of a future that overcame the racially divided present they were made in. The future became unimaginable—other than a new jetpack for Robocop. Even the gentrification plans are always the same: it's always Delta City coming to replace Old Detroit. Doesn't corporate America learn? Can't they work past their "mental diarrhea" and "constipated notions"? *Robocop 3* wants to be revolutionary, wants to inaugurate some revanchist return to the city, but it founders on its inability to imagine a proletarian revolution that actually builds alliances between people, across racial and class divides. The Mothership might offer something revolutionary, but it requires reinvesting in Clinton's project, one that appeals to the visceral, disrupts politeness, and unsettles suburban contentment.

Robocop offers an intensified version of white futures. Between its gallows portrayal of the future of corporate life, where every manager is in desperate need of impressing the Old Man for fear for his or her life, the corporate takeover of a once-diverse city in an effort to replace "crime" with white workers, and the roboticized version of visceral experience in Robocop himself, whiteness is projected into the future as a tightly controlled experience of the self and society. Beyond the corporate and corporeal, there lies the full automation of ED-209, looming as a threat of what the consequences will be for allowing crime and corporate culture to run amok. The other side of control is domination through automation. P-Funk offers an alternative to this intensification of control, this roboticized viscerality; funk in all its viscous feeling, all its affective disruption, with it raunchy humor and weirdness in its lyrics and music, seeks to reconnect people with the world they inhabit, and with their surprising and unsettling possibilities. If *Robocop* offers a view of desire as always historical—Robocop's longing for the suburban family he lost, the Old Man's efforts to restore the homeliness of Old Detroit—then P-Funk offers a model of desire that revels in its abjection. Playing with bodies as Clinton does—the effluvia of snot, excrement, and urine, and the sexual desires that connect bodies in more than heterosexually monogamous ways—intensifies the abject qualities of the body in an attempt to disrupt tendencies toward control. It might not be enough, though. The forces that *Robocop* seeks to critique are the same that led to Clinton's eventual financial and legal troubles, and by the mid-1980s the future seemed certain to be tightly controlled, its visceral pleasures few and highly scripted. P-Funk's revolution without a manifesto wasn't sufficient, nor was *Robocop*'s easily coopted critique; the system persisted and was likely to intensify along predictable lines.

The Revolutionary Horizons of Labor and Automation: *Blue Collar* and *Player Piano*

SMOKEY WAS KILLED by a malfunctioning car-painting robot. One of his coworkers locked him in the room where the painting robot worked. That nameless coworker then purposefully parked a forklift to block the door. On the busy shop floor, Smokey's screams couldn't be heard over the noises made by the other machines, and by the time he broke through the small window in the door to let fresh air into the room where he was locked, it was too late: he had already asphyxiated. Smokey's death is awful to watch. He is covered in blue paint, coughing, trying to protect himself with a meager rag. He had been duped into the situation by a coworker, entering it without awareness of the possibility that he would soon be dead; it was just a banal part of his daily work until the robot is unresponsive to his attempts to turn it off. And then it's horrific. The tools of his trade turn against him, his coworkers have turned against him, and when his bosses find out about his death, they shrug it off as a workplace accident. Smokey's death is a figuration of the death of the American industrial worker at the hand of automation as forecast in the 1970s, but with the complicit actions of coworkers and managers. The robots are coming, but they won't be science-fictional androids with consciousness. Instead, they'll be mundane, everyday robots that are extensions of the interests of the humans who made them; they'll be intensifications of the desires built into their programming. Their behaviors are predictable, even when they go awry. And the robots both make a change in society inevitable and impossible. Inevitable in that humans will slowly be decentered from the means that they have been given,

41

by those in power, to find meaning in their lives through value-producing labor. Impossible in that they will obscure the power relations that exist between workers in a class system that make this way of life—of finding meaning through producing capitalist value—seem hegemonic. Robots make the necessary revolution impossible—and yet automation itself becomes a site of resistance, obscuring the systems that robots embody.

Smokey's death is a narrative pivot in Paul Schrader's *Blue Collar* (1978), a film that follows three workers, Smokey, Jerry, and Zeke, as they hatch an ill-conceived plan to rob their union's office, stealing the dues payments of their fellow union workers to pay their mounting bills. Living in Detroit at the tail end of the 1970s, Smokey and his friends benefit from the widespread availability of blue-collar jobs, which provide them with steady middle-class incomes. But they find that those incomes aren't enough when raising children, owning a home, and trying to have a little fun on their nights off. Jerry's teenage daughter needs expensive braces, Zeke has been caught in a tax fraud scheme of his own making, and Smokey has a lifestyle to maintain, with fancy furniture and cocaine. They could have just stuck to their jobs, taken out bank loans, and cut their family spending, but the union office seemed like such easy prey. It's only when they break in that they realize there's little cash on hand. Instead, they find accounting books that point to the union's involvement with organized crime. One unwise, desperate scheme hatches another, as Zeke decides to blackmail the union leaders. Jerry and Smokey dissent from the plan, leading to Smokey's death and Jerry turning to the state for protection. Zeke, meanwhile, is paid off by the union by being given a promotion to shop foreman, ensuring that he will stay silent now that he also benefits from the collusion among the union, organized crime, and the corporation itself. Such is the death of solidarity among workers, as Schrader imagines it: murder, rejection, resignation, and cooption are the paths available to labor, and none of them lead to a revolutionary politics that will fundamentally change how labor is organized or how people find meaning in their lives.

Schrader's canny use of a benign, killer robot captures American fears about automation and how it will disrupt the suburban, middle-class idyll that widespread industrial jobs provided for many American workers in the twentieth century. Today, Smokey's death would be at the hands of his smartphone, brought about by a malignant but clueless algorithm based on his Amazon purchases. Erik Brynjolfsson and Andrew McAfee's *The Second Machine Age* (2014) captures the same fear, but in the present. They see the inevitability of human workers being replaced by automatons of all sorts, from manufacturing jobs where robots will take over most repetitive tasks to artificial intelligences that will be able to analyze medical scans and create media content. No one is safe from automation in the Second Machine Age, just as no one was actually safe during the First Machine Age. After all, Karl Marx and Frederick Engels then warned that "entire sections of the ruling classes are, by the advance of industry, precipitated into the proletariat" (Marx and Engels 1998, 47). Industry, by its very nature, makes larger and larger swathes of human labor redundant. The transition to automated workforces depends both on a mechanistic understanding of human labor, from manual, repetitive blue-collar work, to creative, intellectual white-collar work. It also recognizes that labor that depends on the refinement of the senses—from a radiologist reading an x-ray to a sommelier recommending wine—can all be programmed into machines. Even economic analysis and the writing of books is subject to the powers of automation, as artificial intelligences grow "smarter" through adaptive learning (Heckman 2008), the amassing of already-existing media, and the possibilities to act in unforeseen and creative ways. What will we do when the robots take our jobs? In the Second Machine Age, Brynjolfsson and McAfee recommend, first, that we educate ourselves and our future generations to ensure that they work in jobs that are resilient to automation; beyond that, they recommend that we levy taxes on those corporations who would seek to automate labor, ensuring that individuals either keep their jobs—being cheaper than robots and their

attendant taxes—or that a basic income is provided to all those
workers that are made redundant by robot labor. But the problem
they see is an old one: humans find meaning through their labor,
and the transition to an automated workforce will be a difficult for
them precisely because of this dependence on labor to craft their
subjectivities. The loss of labor will be deflating, creating a listless class of robot resenters who would more likely revolt against
their robot replacements than the corporations who installed the
robots in the first place. Such a failure of imagination! Why is it
so difficult to imagine a Second Machine Age that once and for all
liberates us from the toils of work, from the necessity of finding
meaning through the corporations that control the means of production in modern life?

At the heart of Kurt Vonnegut's *Player Piano* (2006) is precisely
this question. Vonnegut's speculative novel follows Paul Proteus,
an engineer who oversees the automated production of a factory
in a fictional city in upstate New York. Paul is torn: at once he finds
his job rewarding, but he feels alienated—in the classic Marxist
sense. His work has divorced him from nature, and he seeks to
establish a balance with a more natural, less automated life. He
moves his wife from their secure, upper-middle-class home in
the suburbs of Ilium to a country home where they experiment
with making butter in a churn and live without the conveniences
of modern life as they know it. This leads to marital strife and an
eventual divorce, but Paul is undeterred. Instead, he falls in with
a revolutionary movement—a group of former workers who live
listless lives now that they have been displaced from their jobs by
full automation. In their uprising against the machines, with a riot
that leads them into the factories where they once worked, they
smash the robots that have replaced them; they also riot throughout the city, destroying every robot they find, from innocuous food-
vending machines to telephones. Paul and the other leaders of the
Ghost Shirt Society decide that "they would make the ruins a laboratory, a demonstration of how well and happily men could live with
virtually no machines. . . . 'All right, so we'll heat our water and cook

our food and light and warm our homes with wood fires'.... 'And walk wherever we're going'.... 'And read books instead of watching television'" (Vonnegut 2006, 336). Their Luddite victory is short lived, however. As they pick their way through the city, they stumble into the train station where a group of people is standing around an Orange-O drink dispenser. There they find two men working to rehabilitate the Orange-O machine and a line of interested people waiting for their drinks. Paul recognizes one of the men working on the machine, a "tall, middle-aged, ruddy-faced man who'd fixed Paul's car with the sweatband of his hat long ago. The man had been desperately unhappy then. Now he was proud and smiling because his hands were busy doing what they liked to do best, Paul supposed—replacing men like himself with machines" (338). What Paul recognizes in this mechanic is a will to tinker, a desire to engineer, which will mean that all of the smashed machines will be repaired in time, new machines will be fashioned, and the fantasy of a technology-free life will be unattainable. The revolution fails, precisely because it doesn't destroy the system in its entirety; it simply inverts who is in power, from the elite engineers to the out-of-work proletariat. But once the proletariat assumes power, they just become engineers. The system persists, and there's no displacing it. As one of Paul's co-conspirators remarks, "This isn't the end, you know . . . Nothing ever is, nothing ever will be—not even Judgment Day" (341). History repeats and the revolution will happen again and again, but the system will remain in place. The system is dependent, and formed from, the tinkering spirit, that will to make life more comfortable with machines, even though the outcome will be dissatisfaction with a life freed from labor.

The problem—for Zeke in *Blue Collar*, for the workers in Ilium, for Brynjolfsson and McAfee, is that they cannot conceive of life outside of this system, which depends on domination of workers through their labor, and that is supported by the institutions that compose industrial, and postindustrial, society. Like Marx and Engels argue, the problem with capitalism is that, eventually, everyone is out of a job. But this is only an actual problem to the extent that working is a necessity for being able to live. If needs could be met through automation taxes and other governmental attempts to ensure the livelihood of those who have been displaced from the workforce, then there is the possibility of labor being separable from living. This is a speculative reality that William Morris elaborated in his socialist utopia *News from Nowhere* (1993), first published in 1890 and imagining the world of 2090. The intervening centuries have seen a total social revolution, stemming from the inadequacies of industrial capitalism to meet the needs of individuals, foremost among them the need for rest. Central to the lifestyles of our successors is the harnessing of technologies that automate "irksome" work. As Morris's utopian historian explains to the protagonist visiting from Morris's time period,

> All work which would be irksome to do by hand is done by immensely improved machinery; and in all work which it is a pleasure to do by hand machinery is done without. There is no difficulty in finding work which suits the special turn of mind of everybody; so that no man is sacrificed to the wants of another. From time to time, when we found out that some piece of work was too disagreeable or troublesome, we have given it up and done altogether without the thing produced by it. Now, surely you can see that under these circumstances all the work that we do is an exercise of the mind and body more or less pleasant to be done: so that instead of avoiding work everybody seeks it. (Morris 1993, 127)

Morris changes the problem from a threat of automation taking all jobs to automation freeing individuals from undesirable work, allowing them to invest their time in labor that they find pleasurable. This leads to a resurgence of the arts and sciences, as they no longer exist solely in the context of capitalist production and exchange and can be pursued by everyone equally. Work becomes a challenge, not a chore, and even for those who desire to make salable goods, the drive toward durable, aesthetically pleasing objects entails a move away from alienating mass production and toward an attention to the careful production of goods. As Morris's historian explains, "Again, as more and more pleasure is imported into work, I think we shall take up kinds of work which produce desirable wares, but which we gave up because we could not carry them on pleasantly" (128). Morris's future is regressive, finding a return to pre-industrial social forms preferable to a more technologized one, but the technologies that he allows, discrete as they are, free people from meaningless labor.

Morris's historian singles out the United States as particularly devastated as a result of industrial capitalism, noting that

> Especially the northern parts of America, suffered so terribly from the full force of the last days of civilization, and became such horrible places to live in, that they are now very backward in all that makes life pleasant. . . . the people of the northern parts of America have been engaged in gradually making a dwelling-place out of a stinking dust-heap; and there is still a great deal to do, especially as the country is so big. (128)

Morris's description of what's left of the United States, a postapocalyptic landscape brought about by industrialization, a country "so big," calls for a revolution of a different sort. What's often missing in Morris's sociological imagination—despite trenchant critiques of British imperialism—is attention to race in the making and sustenance of the capitalist system of domination through labor. Here, then, Malcolm X might provide a theory of the necessary revolution, one that depends equally on capitalist exploitation and the use of race in intra- and interclass antagonisms. In his founding lecture to the Organization for Afro-American Unity, Malcolm X argues, "It's the system that is rotten; we have a rotten system. It's a system of exploitation, a political and economic system of exploitation, of outright humiliation, degradation, discrimination—all of the negative things that you can run into, you have run into under this system that disguises itself as a democracy" (X 1970, 73–74). Malcolm X's theory of revolutionary politics is different from Morris's—and, by extension, from that of many theorists in the Marxian tradition, which would not be a return to a precapitalist form of life but an overturning of the system altogether. He theorizes that "a revolution changes the system, it destroys the system and replaces it with a better one. It's like a forest fire . . . it burns everything in its path.

And the only way to stop a forest fire from burning down your house is to ignite a fire that you control and use it against the fire that is burning out of control" (X 1970, 34–35). Those in power already understand the hydraulic nature of politics, he suggests, having successfully thwarted the revolution that should be happening in Malcolm X's moment, and, again, in our own. Infighting and mis-recognition help to ensure that the revolution never gets off the ground, it never truly alights, leaving the system in place, and, po-tentially, creating the fantasy of the possibility of a return to a pre-industrial state where there is no danger of automation, and where labor retains its capitalist-derived meaning.

Blue Collar is a film about Detroit, and, in so being, about la-bor as a function of the industrial capitalist system on the eve of automation. Its central relationship, between three working-class men, two black, one white, stages the counterrevolutionary pol-itics that Malcolm X so perfectly captures in the metaphor of a fire set to counteract the potential of a revolution in the making. Zeke, Smokey, and Jerry have seized the means to revolutionize labor—they have the possibility to expose the union for the cor-rupt organization that it is, as well as the negligence at the heart of American corporate social forms. Admittedly, it's unlikely that the information they've collected from the union office will be enough to overturn the entire capitalist system as they know it, but, as a token of a possible revolutionary politics, their story exposes how counterrevolutionary tactics rely on racial and class situations in the United States to ensure that the revolution never occurs. Each of the men becomes convinced that the others are threats to their well-being, and rather than articulate a politics of their collective interests, which might lie in the revolutionary overthrow of a cor-rupt organization, they each seek their own personal gain. In so doing, they keep the system in place, ensuring that its "humilia-tion, degradation, [and] discrimination" favors thinking of oneself, and personal gain remains the basis for worker subjectivity. In *Player Piano,* rather than relying on the interpersonal to thwart revolutionary politics, robots serve to deflect critique, while also serving as a screen for human desires. A return to work, with all of its "irksome" labor, is seemingly preferable to a life where all necessities are met, precisely because people haven't been prepared for a life without work. Automation seems to be the problem, but the real problem is that capitalism has depended on a system of "humiliation, degradation, [and] discrimination" that leaves the out-of-work individual listless and unable to imagine a "pleasant" form of labor—like Morris's appeal to a more participatory art and science, or even the aesthetic production of goods. The problem that Malcolm X identifies is the systemic nature of the problem; no one part can change and result in a more equitable society. Without the total transformation of the system, it will persist. The future never comes; it is merely the intensification of the past, relying on already-existing relationships and fears. The system remains. Until it burns down.

California Diaries, 2008–2015

WE LIVED IN CALIFORNIA for the better part of a decade. Moving from the American Midwest, my partner and I had to learn how to dread a new, geographically particular set of futures. First, there were the earthquakes. Everyone assured us that earthquakes were no big deal—except when they were, like during the Loma Prieta earthquake in 1989. But there was nothing to do about earthquakes since they just happened. You could buy over-expensive insurance to help rebuild a home, but everyone assured us that any significant earthquake would necessitate the U.S. government getting involved, and FEMA would save us since we had the benefits of structural racism and wealth on our side, unlike those pulverized by Hurricane Katrina. Then there were the ever-looming wildfires, evidence of which we could see hovering over the mountains to the north of us in the summer of 2008, and which we would sometimes catch a glimpse of as we flew home from out of state, far from the coast, high in the mountains. But, again, there was nothing to be done about wildfires since they just happened. You could clear the dry brush from your yard; you could make sure that your home stood apart from anything that might catch it on fire. Someone else built our house, and we did our best to keep the yard clear, but a fire always seemed like a looming possibility, since the grass was so dry and the undergrowth so brittle. And then there was the possibility of a tidal wave or sea-level rise, but we seemed well protected in our mountain home, some four hundred feet above sea level. Sure, we'd be living in a new archipelago, and would have to take up sailing to commute to the grocery store and work, but at least the house would be intact. Over time, we attuned ourselves to a much more manageable catastrophe: invasive plants.

Through national tragedy and personal good fortune, we were able to buy a home in Santa Cruz County. The Great Recession led to homes being marginally less expensive, and the combination of inheritance and parental support made it possible to buy a home with an affordable mortgage. For my partner and I, this would be the first time we were homeowners rather than renters, and we took to the care of our property with a seriousness that we had previously lacked. Not that we were disrespectful to our earlier landlords, but rather we could now invest in creating a domestic vision, including landscaping our yard and gardening. Moving to California from the Midwest meant attuning ourselves to a very different environment of plants. Seduced by the arboretum at the University of California, Santa Cruz, we first started to experiment with plants suitable to the climate that were imports from similar agricultural zones—from South Africa, New Zealand, and Australia. Their alienness was alluring. Through our own ineptitude, many of these early investments in our yard failed—too much or too little water, and not enough protection from local pests (including gophers, who I would learn to truly hate). We were slowly steered toward what we learned were "native" plants by the horticulturalists we met. Native plants have a long history that dovetails with nativist, ethnocentric movements in the United States and elsewhere, but we were unaware of those histories when we started to plant native buckwheats and lilacs in our yard. We imagined that we were helping to foster a return of sorts for our yard and for the local environment. The flipside of our active planting efforts was staying attuned to possible invasive species. French broom, Chinese Trees of Heaven, black locust. We learned to spot their sprouts, and yank them from the soil before they could gain too strong a footing. The future, we were told by our local gardening experts and fellow landowners, was at risk: if we failed to be vigilant about these invaders, not only would our yard be overcome with undesirable aliens, but the natives we had grown in our affection would lose their place as well. We came to see the native plants in our yard and in our local environment as precariously holding on. In that way, these modest plants and our modest domestic project became metonymic of life in California. Everything felt so precarious, so subject to change. More than once, while walking our dogs through the neighborhood, I stopped to pull an errant French broom. The future, after all, was at stake.

In California, the future seemed so perilous. And yet it was also so abstract and unknowable. Yes, most of it was mediated for us—through videos of earthquakes and wildfires, in viral magazine pieces about the looming tidal wave that would devastate the Pacific Northwest, in economic measures that made clear what risks California was becoming more exposed to, like bankruptcy due to the cost of fighting wildfires. Meanwhile, we slowly became aware of the very real economic disparities in the state and the impacts these had on everything from public education to housing. We slowly became aware of how the risks associated with all of the coming catastrophes were unevenly distributed across the population, based more on economic comfort than geography or preparedness. I reflected from time to time on a tour of the area that I had been given by a senior coworker: as we drove through a part of town called Beach Flats—which was literally that, a near sea-level neighborhood adjacent to the beach—she told me that mostly Latinos lived there. What she didn't say was that with sea-level rise the neighborhood would turn into a lagoon, and those families would all be displaced. Our once-mountain, future-archipelago home would be largely immune from the same event. Similarly, the families who couldn't afford costly private schools were forced to send their children to increasingly crowded public schools or homeschool them. The culprit at the root of it all was Proposition 13, a law passed by California voters in 1978 that capped property tax at 1 percent of the value of a home and also stopped the reassessment of home values unless they were sold. As long as the same owner retained a property, the property tax was assessed at 1978 levels, with minor changes for inflation over time and market forces. Homes could pass down through families to avoid being reassessed, with parents transferring titles to children. Meanwhile, those new to the state paid market value for homes—and the reassessed cost of property taxes. Economic disparity was written into the very legal basis of the state and perpetuated the inequities and precarities unevenly distributed across communities.

"Neoliberalism" is what we call it (Harvey 2005). At once, the term is used to describe the economic policies that have led to the privatization of once-public goods—from state universities and public health care to national parks now seen as untapped oil reserves—and the modes of subjection that increasingly focus on the importance of the individual and his or her powers of self-determination. These transformations, or intensifications, built upon the turn toward financialization of the market in the 1970s—away from the dependency on material, industrial production and toward speculative investment markets. It also followed on the flight of white urbanites to the growing suburbs, divorcing themselves from the city centers and the diverse communities—economic, sexual, ethnic, and racial—and entrenching elite families in the need to maintain their suburban property values through ensuring that the right kinds of people populated their suburban idylls—no "zombies," thank you very much! The decline of industrial labor also led to a recoding of value in professional preparation: no longer could a high school degree guarantee a lifetime of economic comfort; instead, a college education was now necessary. Individual worth increasingly could be measured through standardized tests mandated by states of students in public schools, and tests like the SAT and ACT helped to ensure that students were properly sorted—based on their intellectual capacities masking their economic privilege—into the right universities, and, eventually, into the right professions. The Prosperity Gospel found itself materialized in the everyday politics of racial and class distinction, meted out through education, property, and the increasingly disparate exposure to risk (Bowler 2013).

About ten years before moving to California, I had read Kim Stanley Robinson's Three Californias trilogy, a loose set of novels depicting parallel possibilities for California, mostly focused on

Orange County, south of Los Angeles. The first, *The Wild Shore* (1984), imagines a postapocalyptic California, returned to an agrarian state as a result of a Soviet attack; the second, *The Gold Coast* (1988), offers what feels like the more realistic future—one in which suburban sprawl has conquered the landscape and people jet from place to place in guided vehicles; and the third, *Pacific Edge* (1990), an idyllic ecotopia that posits a future changed through financial regulation. At the root of each book is a conception of capitalism as a failed cultural and economic system—one that divides nations from each other, individuals from their social and natural environments, and individuals from each other. If there can be said to be a thesis to the trilogy, it is that capitalism is predicated on the economic value of the catastrophe, from the individual to the social to the global. Capitalism, for Robinson, a child of California, is alienating—just like Marx always argued (1992)—and in that alienation gains a foothold into capitalizing on catastrophes.

This is not merely "disaster capitalism"—the ways that capitalist value is produced through the uneven and negligent investments in conditions that expose particular communities to risk (Klein 2007)—but, rather, the situations that capitalism produces through alienation allow for the production of value. Disaster capitalism is procedural; catastrophic capitalism is ontological—it is the basis of capitalism itself. This returns capitalism to the original conception of Marx's understanding of "second nature": the production of the commodity as an industrial product that separates humans from their natural environment and replaces it with an understanding of nature as mediated through industrial production and capitalist exchange. Marx's reimagining of the Edenic fall from grace is one that is predicated on economic transitions in the relationships between individuals, and in the constitution of society itself: it divorces nature from the human realm, fundamentally. And that's the problem across Robinson's Three Californias. Nature has become a resource to be mined, to be built upon, to be capitalized on, and in so doing these human processes further alienate individuals and communities so that when the catastrophic occurs, capital is the only possible solution. This isn't merely making money for some at the expense of others; this is making a worldview meaningful through its ability to save lives, to cohere social relationships, and to restore some sense of order to the world.

The strongest pair, *The Wild Shore* and *Pacific Edge*, attempts to imagine life after the vagaries of American capitalism at the end of the twentieth century. *The Wild Shore* depicts a California rebuilding after warfare, and *Pacific Edge* imagines a California rebuilding after an economic catastrophe. In *Pacific Edge*, something devastating has happened in the early 2000s leading to the enactment of a set of regulations regarding the size of corporations and the pay disparities allowed within a business. This is all motivated by a growing recognition—it seems—that the Earth provides finite resources, and a more ecologically conscious politics is necessary to steward the planet and maintain the human population. This means limiting the growth of cities based on the resources available, and those resources are controlled by the state. Robinson rolls back the privatization of neoliberalism, creating a communitarian-market society, one in which community members work ten hours in weekly support of the needs of the community, thereby limiting the size of government through volunteerism. But the profit motive is never truly eradicated, and the central tension of the novel is based on the desires of some community members to broker a deal with international real estate interests to sell a nature preserve for suburban development—presumably with kickbacks provided to the American brokers. The idyll of El Modena, where softball and Jacuzzi baths seem to be a way of life, where social mobility is possible and education and health care are provided for all, still isn't enough for some, who see the possibility for personal enrichment through capital. Capital is the problem, and even when it is reimagined in *Pacific Edge*, it is still impoverished as a way to relate to one's community, to other individuals, and to nature.

To keep returning to capitalism as a social form and cultural system when it is predicated on the catastrophic relation of individuals to their world is the very basis of an abusive relationship. Capitalism sets the conditions of catastrophe and yet it is returned to again and again as the basis for understanding social relations and subjectivity—that is the very seed of liberalism, and, again, in neoliberalism, both of which center the individual as the basis for social relations, for identity and self-conception, and as a governing principle. Robinson's apocalypses aren't total enough—they don't extinguish capitalism and its influences on people, including the desires that it creates. Consider Ursula K. Le Guin's position and solution: she too seems to consider capitalism invidious, and only through its total removal can some form of true communitarianism be developed. This is the basis for *The Dispossessed* (1994), which, allegorically, depicts Earth circa 1974. The global powers in Le Guin's novel are locked in a Cold War of sorts, with capitalism on one side of the divide and party socialism on the other, but the socialists are as bad as the capitalists, trapped by their understandings of economics and individual self-worth. Into this bipolar set of ideologies comes Shevik, an emissary from a distant moon, where an experiment in anarcho-communitarianism has taken place over the last two hundred years. Raised on a world where there is no system of economic abstraction—no imposition of exchange or symbolic value over the use value of persons or things—the worst thing you can be on the anarcho-communitarian moon Annarres is self-interested. Despite looking like those around him on the capitalism-trapped Urras, Shevik is a true alien: what he believes, his whole system of conceptualizing the social and an individual's role within it, is absolutely unknowable for those who have grown up in a world shaped by the value systems of capitalism—which, inherently, reify the role of the individual and the need for self-interest.

It's hard not to read Le Guin and Robinson as both critiquing the anticapitalist pretenses of California in the 1960s as a leader in the then-counterculture movement. For all the critiques of capitalism that came out of the 1960s, none could unwind the effects of individualism in American society. The individual, as a way to conceptualize the self but also one's relationship to society and systems of value, was so entrenched that regardless of how the individual was critiqued, by the 1970s, this communitarian alternative had become a "culture of narcissism" (Lasch 1979), one in which self-help had come to replace communes and retreats, and food cooperatives had become "health food" stores. Rather than the state where capitalism went to die, foundering on the edge of the American frontier, California became the state where capitalism became intensified into property-interested libertarianism. The combined forces of Central Valley agro-business, Hollywood and the Los Angeles media industry, and Bay Area Silicon Valley produced wealth enough for Californians to imagine that they could transcend capitalism, or at least secede from the United States. Yet, the actual effect was that above all else, property ruled. And individual relationships to and through property managed the relations between individuals and the world around them.

This, then, was the California we inherited from the generations before us. Less a state of "we're all in this together" than "every man, woman, and child for themselves." Or, at least, "every family for itself." That reality could be obscured depending on one's position, quite literally in one's geography, but more often through class ideologies. The same community could be cut through along class lines, totally unseen due to the generational gifts of property that sustained families staying in otherwise too-expensive areas. We upper-middle-class academics, buoyed with family inheritance, beneficiaries of centuries of privilege associated with whiteness, found ourselves neighbors to families just scraping by while living in homes they struggled to buy and maintain payments on, other families who had been living in the same home for the past forty years, beneficiaries of Proposition 13, and families that had passed down the same home from generation to generation. On a class level, this made the area highly diverse. And yet, everyone was white. The one black person in the neighborhood was a child adopted by white parents. That nearly complete blanket of whiteness produced the appearance of a shared community, but the reality was that children were being subtly sorted into overenrolled public schools versus the private, $16,000-tuition Montessori elementary schools. Some families were able to maintain the upkeep on their homes, replacing dilapidated roofing or installing solar panels, while other families cobbled together home repairs in an attempt to maintain their property values. You see where this all is going, right? On the one hand there were those who were economically festooned—they were going to be just fine no matter what. On the other, there were those who had much more obviously precarious lives, piecing together work and resources as they could in the hopes that one day their children would be able to inherit their ever-growing-in-value home. But, regardless of who had what, the possibility that a devastating catastrophe could lay them all low lingered; an earthquake, a tsunami, a wildfire—they were indiscriminate in their effects. And then it was every man, woman, or child for him- or herself. Well, unless it was a FEMA-level disaster, and then it would be every man, woman, or child supported by the state—a state that Californian libertarianism would otherwise hold in contempt through a refusal to pay adequate property taxes to support everyone equally.

Yesterday's countercultural hippies and dropouts had become today's property value–protecting suburbanites. This wasn't just young Democrats turning into old Republicans, deeply invested in protecting their social safety net after years of paying taxes into entitlement programs; it was young critics of American capitalism and its construction of the individual turned into old Libertarians, invested not only in the individual as a self that could benefit from "self-improvement" but also one who believed in the intrinsic value of property, the entitlement one has to benefits of property ownership, and the need to protect one's property from the actions of others. What community might have been spawned by communes and community agricultural programs foundered on the protectionist, individualist logics of those who had seen their property's value increase steadily over the decades since Proposition 13. Despite liberal social views, the rise in property values drove regressive economic positions that produced and entrenched class relations that benefited those who were landed thanks to the Republican movements in the state in the 1970s— including the governorship of Ronald Reagan, that great neoliberalist, and the middle-of-the-road politics of Jerry Brown. What had the appearance of a liberal social democracy was actually a libertarian experiment in the collective distrust of the state—in refusing taxes as much as it was about determining who could marry whom through marriage equality, and whether it was legal to grow marijuana for "medicinal" use. And yet the two worldviews, social democracy and property-based libertarianism, could—and often did—exist side by side without contradiction, which, especially to the outside, makes it appear as if California is at the forefront of liberal democracy. What it's really at the forefront of is neoliberalism rooted in libertarian ideologies of the individual and property and a refusal of state power.

By the time we left California, it came as something of a relief. I wouldn't have to think about the leak in our roof any longer—a worry granted to me by the generations of people who had lived in our home before us, each economically unable to repair the roof completely, and an anxiety that persisted despite the years of drought that we lived through. And, for us, it was always next year's repair to invest in—if we were, in fact, going to make a life in California in the long term. That's generationality for you: one generation bestowing unto the next its many burdens, making the next the same as the last in an endless progression of sameness. One generation's anxiety becomes the next's, and so on, and so on. I lay in bed, thinking not of nuclear Armageddon but the leak in the roof. Because that was an anxiety I could manage. The catastrophes would catch us all, but maybe I could fix the leak, and make sure that all those invasive plants knew their place wasn't in our yard. And maybe, on a walk with the dogs, I could take a minute and pull up some errant French broom. For nature. Or for property values.

Extrapolating Neoliberalism in the Western Frontier: Octavia Butler's Parables

"CHANGE IS GOD," Lauren Olamina tells us in the first pages of Octavia Butler's *Parable of the Sower* (1993). Olamina starts the Earthseed series young in years—just in her teens—but mature in her self-conception and understanding of the world around her. She lives with her parents and siblings in a small neighborhood enclave in Robledo, outside of Los Angeles. Her parents both teach, her father for the nearby university, her mother offering an in-home school for the kids in the neighborhood. Olamina knows enough to keep her poetic, theosophical writing to herself, writing in journals that she hides; her vaguely New Age-y, thoroughly disorganized attempts at religion are too controversial for her parents to bear. But at the heart of Olamina's nascent religion is the idea that God isn't embodied in a particular personage or prophet but is an ongoing process. God is creation, change, transformation; God is operating all the time in small and big ways. There's no reason to be angry at God, because, ultimately, God is changing things for change's sake, not for the benefit or detriment to any individual. God just happens. Olamina's writings take shape over her teenage years, and when her natal home burns down, claiming her family, she sets out on a road trip—on foot—from Los Angeles to northern California. Along the way, her little religion, Earthseed, begins to attract followers, until they collectively found a religious community on an abandoned farm. Earthseed, like capitalism, is predicated on change; for capitalism, it comes in the form of "creative destruction"; for Earthseed it seems to be much the same.

At the heart of the Earthseed novels are two inexorable forces that reappear throughout Butler's work: human nature and capitalism. Human nature, for Butler, is selfish and mean. It is probably best captured in the institution of American slavery, which she wrote about throughout her career, sometimes veiled, other times quite explicitly. At its heart, slavery for Butler is about one person subjugating another for no other reason than the gain of the master. There's no romance in the institution of slavery, nothing more than human nature reduced to its barest expression of self-interest at the expense of others, meted out through violence. And this is also the basis of capitalism for Butler, bent to the interests of the wealthy at the expense of the laboring middle and lower classes. Capitalism, for Butler, is the bare expression of self-interest, driving those who are wealthy to not only exploit laborers but to ensure their blindness to the lived experiences of those they extract wealth from. Butler's view of human nature and capitalism are inextricable from her experiences as a black American born in the twentieth century before the passage of Civil Rights, and whose young adulthood and adulthood were spent in the shadow of its passage and the long wake it produced. This is not to reduce Butler's social theory to her biography but to suggest that what produced the foundation for her theorizations of human action and social institutions was an understanding of humans as being motivated by their self interests, desires that were refracted through the institutions created and sustained by those in power—who happened to be beneficiaries of centuries of American capitalism founded on the institution of slavery. Setting the Earthseed novels—at least initially—in California is a way to think through the relationship of these drives in the context of the American frontier, particularly as a form of extrapolation, where the plot of the Earthseed novels relies, fundamentally, on the projection of past forces into the future.

Frederick Jackson Turner, a historian of the American West, writing in the nineteenth century when the West was still east of the Mississippi, imagined that what the frontier provided was a temporal laboratory (Turner 1998). Turner suggests that as one follows American settlements westward, from New York through Ohio, and eventually past the Mississippi, one can see earlier moments of civilization at work. From the high transatlantic influences apparent in New York City, each settlement westward takes one back to an earlier stage of civilizational development, making apparent, at each stop, a move away from lawfulness and the deliberate ordering of society toward less lawful and more violent possibilities. From civilization, one moves back to barbarism, and toward outright savagery on the edge of the frontier. Such a view legitimates the use of violence on the frontier, between settlers but also against indigenous populations—there is no civilization to bar such violence. Such a view also depends on an understanding of civilization as a unilineal outcome of a progressive set of social stages, which is a teleological conception of the ideals and practices of Turner's contemporary world as being the natural outcome of a drive toward precisely those ends. This conception of "unilineal evolution," popular in Turner's time and informed by social Darwinism, was the false belief that societies, like species, evolved over time to be more efficient and more functional. Unlike species, the theory of unilineal evolution held that societies also became better and fairer, more rational, less superstitious, less bound by kinship and more egalitarian. But even a casual understanding of Turner's time—and our own—immediately raises questions about how civilized any given society is. The frontier, for Turner, and often in speculative fiction, is a time-space machine—it allows people to imagine what the future looks like, and sometimes what the past might have looked like too. It also, in the words of Robert Heinlein, provides a way to think about "if this goes on" (Heinlein 1940)—what the present will look like if extrapolated into the future with few changes and the increased centrality of once-underlying forces—like human nature and capitalism—as the basis of society.

The frontier that Butler imagines California being plays with Turner's conception of the frontier as a time-space machine:

California is a stage in the future, not in the past, and a stage that extrapolates from already-existing trends to their logical bases as catastrophes for society. One of the narrators of *Parable of the Talents* (1998), Laruen Olamena's partner, Bankole, tells us that

> I have read that the period of upheaval that journalists have begun to refer to as "the Apocalypse" or more commonly, more bitterly, "the Pox," lasted from 2015 through 2030—a decade and a half of chaos. This is untrue. The Pox has been a much longer torment. It began well before 2015, perhaps before the turn of the millennium. It has not ended.
>
> I have also read that the Pox was caused by accidentally coinciding climatic, economic, and sociological crises. It would be more honest to say that the Pox was caused by our own refusal to deal with obvious problems in those areas. We caused the problems: then we sat and watched as they grew into crises. . . . All too often, [wars during this period] were actually fought because inadequate leaders did not know what else to do. Such leaders knew that they could depend on fear, suspicion, hatred, need, and greed to arouse patriotic support for war. (1998, 14)

Bankole's assessment is straightforward enough: it wasn't one thing, a single catastrophe, that tipped society into the postapocalyptic world he now inhabits, but the combined forces of economic, social, and climatic changes—the latter presumably driven by the former two. Capitalism is at the heart of each of these forces, and the near catastrophes that it allows created the foundation on which their combined systemic failures could produce the apocalypse that they do. Olamina's United States is a bleak place: neighborhoods have been surrounded by protective walls and subsist as much as possible on homegrown produce. Inflation has run rampant, and Olamina's professor father brings home barely enough money to support his family in their modest home; what was once a squarely upper-middle-class income has become poverty-line scraping by. Work of all kinds is scarce—both the industrial manufacturing base and the "creative class" have been eviscerated by the full neoliberalization of the economy. Whole U.S. cities are sold to corporations in the apotheosis of privatization—all because corporations promise full employment to those who would remain in the sold city, which will ultimately depend on new forms of indenture that span across generations. Social services provided by the state—education, policing, firefighting, emergency paramedics—have all eroded to the point where they either have disappeared or are susceptible to corruption. Rampant homelessness has led to a new class of the dispossessed, roamers who use violence to take what they want from those who have it. Meanwhile, the wealthiest members of society have retreated to armed compounds where new forms of slavery provide them with the servants they need to work their farms and maintain their property. As Bankole narrates, there's nothing new here: this is the United States readers are familiar with, just taken to ends that expose the social, economic, and climatic tensions we tend to collectively suppress—except in moments of upheaval. And the Pox is that: an ongoing dissolution of U.S. society to the point that it becomes lawless and inchoate. What was once California, Oregon, and Washington has become three separate nation-states, each desperate to protect its borders and operating without federal support. The West has become the frontier again.

Like the last time, in the eighteenth and nineteenth centuries, this time the frontier is a playground for capitalism and the worst human impulses. And, it seems, even the transcendent promise of Earthseed can't really shake these influences. Earthseed promises that the future of humanity lies in the stars, and Butler had planned a series of sequels that would follow groups of colonists on their settler-colonial missions into space, where, each time, they would find a planet just barely hospitable to human life. Each planet would have enough to support human life, but nothing as beautiful or bountiful as Earth; and, nowhere, it seems, based on her notes, would planetary conditions allow for a system like capitalism to take hold. One recurrent setting for these projected novels was the world of Bow, a world characterized by its grey, drab color scheme, with the one glimmer of beauty being occasional rainbows, from which the planet derives its name. Bow offers little more than subsistence levels for life there, and no one person can get a foothold to begin exploiting the labor of others or the environment; capital-ism, Butler suggests, is predicated on the possibility of abundance and is a natural outcome of Earth's environment in which there is enough abundance to enable some to horde resources without entirely depriving others in their world to the point of starvation. Instead, the abundance of Earth plays into the production of a particular human nature, one that builds upon the possibilities of selfishness and the power-hungry control of others epitomized in the institution of slavery but obvious throughout capitalist forms. Butler's notes on her possible sequels suggest that the old, easy impulses toward individualism and the domination of others that Earthly capitalism enabled wouldn't be possible on Bow. Instead, the only way that the Earthseed community would survive would be through radical experiments in communitarianism.

To force the issue, Butler imagines a host of possible afflictions to bring the community together. The most tantalizing is a blind-ness that strikes the whole community, which, over time, resolves into the telepathic ability to see through other people's eyes but not one's own. This communitarian clairvoyance could not be any more explicit in its literalism, not unlike Wyndham's use of blind-ness in *Day of the Triffids*. For Butler, it's an expression of "our own refusal to deal with obvious problems." The only way that we can overcome that blindness is through a reliance on others—to, at least metaphorically, see through one another's eyes. In that context, it's important that Olamina is a "hyperempath," the Larmarckian effect of a pharmaceutically induced birth defect that allows her to experience the sensations of others. This allows her, at its best, to experience her partner's sexual pleasure on top of her own; at its worst, she experiences the pain and death of others, which can result in her losing consciousness. It's this hyperempathy, Butler suggests, that allows Olamina to understand what others need, leading her to seek to create it in the form of Earthseed. The reli-gion she slowly crafts, with its emphasis on change and mutability, is intended to provide the solace that individuals and communities need in the face of ongoing structural and interpersonal change, all wrought by capitalism's entrenchment in society, which has shaped humans in particular ways to expect—if not depend on—capitalism as a savior of those in need, all through the recuperative possibilities of creative destruction. Instead, Earthseed intervenes to explain away the need for change as a cosmological effect, and one that only community will step in to help in aiding one's acclimation to emerging situations. Earthseed is not so much a revolution as a substitution: Earthseed takes the place of capitalism without eradicating it. In order to extinguish capitalism entirely, a new environment is necessary—one that will both create the basis of a new social form and make a new kind of person possible as well. These sequels were never completed, and maybe that's fitting: Butler sought to do something truly radical, make something entirely alien, and maybe that was impossible to really imagine, let alone put into prose.

As extrapolation, Butler takes these institutions and forces—neoliberal capitalism, human nature as she views it with its racism and selfishness—and puts them into a future where other forces, like climate change, have intensified. The changes in the climate, which lead to drought and food scarcity, seemingly drive changes in the market as well, with inflation as the result. Alternatively, Butler imagines what these seemingly natural institutions and forces would do in a radically different environment, like the world of Bow. "What if?" undergirds extrapolation, and frames the question and its answer in the context of stable knowns and unstable unknowns, like human nature set loose in a radically different evolutionary environment. In time or in space—or in both—extrapolation asks us to imagine how the institutions and people that make up everyday life in the present will change under radically different circumstances. In so doing, extrapolation seeks to estrange us from the seeming naturalness of those institutions and human behaviors that are so easily taken for granted (Suvin 1979).

For Butler, and for her characters, California doesn't offer a way out of the trap of American capitalism and the venal human nature that it has created. If anything, California offers her a place to imagine what the logical outcomes of those forces will be, given time. And, it wasn't much time at all. The Pox, Bankole recalls, was identified as starting in 2015—a future that we're already living in. Bankole's analysis—that the Pox was a long time coming and enabled by socially produced blindness to the realities of society, the economy, and the environment—suggests that the past of that future is also one we've been living in for a long time. That's the spirit of Robert Heinlein's "if this goes on" kind of extrapolation, taking obvious elements of today's society and extending their implications into the future. Butler's extrapolative powers get her to the point of total collapse: the combined forces that capitalism bring together, the way they become intensified through social blindness, the total erosion of social support, the absolute abandonment of the masses on the part of the government and the wealthy. What Butler has a hard time imagining is what happens next—what a world without capitalism, what a world where this version of human nature is in contradiction to its new environment, would produce. That is less a failure on Butler's part than it is a success of capitalism, which has been so successful in colonizing her—and our—imaginations. That may be the true lesson of Butler's two Parables and their impossible sequels: we can't think ourselves outside of capitalism. The promises of the frontier are not unfettered by or inextricable from capitalism and our collective conceptions of human nature. California is not an escape. Instead, it's very likely the apotheosis of capitalism. Maybe, in its collective catastrophes—earthquakes, wildfires, mudslides, tsunamis, libertarianism, self-help individualism—we can begin to chart a way forward, away from capitalism and its venal human natures and toward something amorphous. In that indeterminacy, we might make new human natures, new social formations, that take us from the traps we find ourselves in and help forge something that creates more rather than fewer possibilities. That's the revolutionary presumption of Earthseed.

New York Diaries, 2015–2018

"SURE BEATS WILDFIRES AND MUDSLIDES!" So jokes my neighbor to me as we shovel the latest winter storm out of our driveways so we can get to work the next day. My response? Those pathetic little laughs that Chris Ware captures so well in his cartoons, a little sad, and not entirely sure that the joke merits a response. I had hoped when we moved to California in 2008 that I would never experience a snowy winter again, and yet here I was, joined in solidarity against winter weather.

For years, I joked with my Californian students that global warming was frightening only to the extent that it appeared to be an actual threat to people. "Global warming" for my extended family in Michigan, like my new neighbors in New York, seemed to be not so bad. Who wouldn't want a slightly warmer winter, even if it comes at the cost of a slightly hotter summer as well? That's nothing air conditioning can't overcome, after all. Thomas Friedman's use of "global weirding" seems to capture our present much better, even if "global warming" is a better description of our eventual shared future. "Weirding" captures the uneven, unpredictable nature of nature as it is being recast as a result of carbon-fuel industrialization and its aftermaths. It properly captures how, on April 5, I can be shoveling a foot of snow from the driveway, while friends in California are finding themselves trapped behind the remnants of mudslides brought down by winter rains—while being told, simultaneously, that their multiyear drought still has not abated. The future will be warmer, and it will also be weirder. Rather than the extrapolative line that futures like Butler's *Parables* offer, or the intensifications of *Robocop*, our shared, weird future is more unpredictable, more impossible, than we tend to imagine. Extrapolation and intensification—however disturbing individual stories may be—are comforting, they play out in ways that are familiar; weird, mutant futures might play on already-existing possibilities, but they are shot through with impossibilities brought into being through our imaginative blindness.

In New York, we bought a home in the floodplain off the Susquehanna River. It's a beautiful old Victorian house, built during the textile boom of the late nineteenth century and lovingly restored by the previous owners. Unlike so many of the homes in the neighborhood where it is located, it has a large yard that runs from the rise on which the home is perched down to the river, affording us a picturesque view of the Susquehanna and the Pocono foothills rising in the distance. I joke to friends that, compared to our old Californian home, it's twice the house for half the price, but that's not so much a joke as an economic analysis of the difference between a place where the future is something that people anticipate, and one where the future seems to never come.

You'd be forgiven for not knowing anything about Binghamton, New York. It's a place defined not so much by itself as by its relations with other places. Located about two hundred miles northwest of New York City, southeast of Buffalo, and north of Philadelphia, Binghamton was a transit hub that, more than a century ago, connected central New York to larger cities for the purpose of moving goods and people. Located at the confluence of the Chenango and Susquehanna rivers, it also served as a means to ship goods downriver to the Chesapeake Bay. As such, Binghamton served as a necessary point for the development of the western frontier in the early expansion of American settler colonialism toward the Great Lakes. That history has long been obscured, with indigenous groups having been relocated to reservations to the north and the west. Like so many cities that exist between other places, Binghamton loses its youth to more vibrant cities. Like so many other cities developed in the early twentieth century under the influence of the personal automobile, it sprawls into its neighbors, with strip malls and big-box stores stretching down a four-lane parkway that follows, roughly, the Susquehanna River. Whatever natural beauty there is is largely obscured by retail spaces, neighborhoods that creep up hillsides, and the looming threat of another catastrophic flood.

Binghamton and its neighbors have had their moments. During the Second World War, the Endicott-Johnson Shoe Company employed some twenty thousand people to make shoes and boots for the American military, turning a regionally respected small business into a major clothing supplier—so successful that it was ultimately bought out after it fell on hard times, moved to Ohio, and its former factories now stand empty. But the arches "erected by workers" that honor the company still stand over Main Street, one on the east side of Johnson City and the other as you enter Endicott to the west. With the benefit of military contracts to support the development of navigation and computing technologies, the Second World War also propelled profits for IBM, which housed one of its factories in nearby Endicott, employing engineers, managers, and industrial workers. The products produced at the Endicott factory resulted in environmental contamination, as the solvents used to clean electronic parts were washed into the river or seeped into the groundwater. The Plume, as this systemic pollution came to be called, was largely composed of trichloroethylene, a substance known to cause cancer, and which could creep up through people's basements, singlehandedly driving down home values throughout Endicott. What was once a modest, middle-class Southern Tier city had become a toxic spill site, its decades of capitalist gain revealed to be a slow, poisonous catastrophe in the making. The Second World War propelled Binghamton to a level of suburban comfort, but over time—as a result of globalization, of industrialization, of stagnation—it has become a strange nowhere zone, a place where the future never seems to come, and the past haunts it in indelible ways, like toxic plumes creeping into people's homes, a return of the repressed, but in a way that Sigmund Freud couldn't imagine (Gordon 1997).

Like so many U.S. cities, convenience stands like a scar across the landscape. Easy shopping, mediocre takeout, and industrially supported grocery stores sprawl from end to end of the parkway. As Amazon and other internet outlets centralize shopping and offer the next level of convenience—why go shopping when delivery is available at the click of a button?—more and more storefronts are emptied. Large department stores that once anchored the local mall, Macy's and Sears, are now empty commercial husks, and there is news that the third of four shopping pillars in the mall will also close. The shopping mall will be a graveyard to quaint, automobile-fueled consumerism, just as the empty factories and warehouses that populate the landscape stand as monuments to a period of industrial production long gone. Over time, the buildings will fall into disrepair; they'll decay, and in their place will be fields of waste that will slowly go wild. But that's a long way off. In the meantime, there's merely resignation, as the future never seems to come, and the past continues to haunt the present.

My favorite thing about Binghamton is Rod Serling, the man who made *The Twilight Zone*. My daily dog walk takes me through a park where a bandstand has been erected in his honor, and a plaque dedicated to him stands in front of the high school. Now, watching his episodes of *The Twilight Zone*, it's hard for me to separate them from this place, a place that often seems depicted in his scripts as a nonplace marked more by memory than any future-oriented pull. "Where Is Everybody?" is both the title of the first episode of "The Twilight Zone" and the slogan on a bumper sticker that I see on my neighbor's car. It feels like such a nonjoke, like my other neighbor's appeal to life without mudslides and wildfires, but it also so perfectly captures the feeling of being in a city that feels vacated of any life, of any presence as a municipal space that people actively participate in. The joke—if it is one—is a strange echo of *The Twilight Zone* episode, where the viewer follows a man through a day in a city that is mysteriously vacant. The protagonist, too, is vacant, seemingly experiencing amnesia, having forgotten his name, where he is, and what he is doing there. The city appears to have been recently vacated—there is still coffee on the stove, still lit cigars that are slowly burning down, lights that go off and on in the daylight and night, movies that start screening without a projectionist. What we come to learn only after the man has a breakdown is that he is part of a simulation of isolation, using a device that is meant to test his ability to withstand social isolation for the time it would take to transport him to the moon and back. The vacant city is something he imagined, not part of the simulation itself, and was presumably the result of a psychotic break. When asked by the commanding officer in charge of the experiment, "Where did you think you were?," he responds "A place I don't want to go again, sir. A town. A town without people, without anybody." The commanding officer goes on to explain that, despite all the technological know-how that will support this astronaut in space, "There's one thing we can't simulate that's a very basic need. Man's hunger for companionship. The barrier of loneliness. That's one thing we haven't licked yet." Although they're talking about the moon and the enforced isolation an individual must face in making the trip—as they imagine it in the mid-1950s—it could also be taken to be an indictment of modern U.S. society. Cities empty of people, and yet all the conveniences remain intact. There's fresh coffee, food to eat, movies to watch, stores full of stuff to buy—for the time being. But there's no "companionship."

If that's too generic, too much a critique of mid-century U.S. society, then consider the episode "Walking Distance," whose story hinges on the presence of a carousel. The fortune made by George Johnson, the industrialist behind the Endicott-Johnson Shoe Company, was spent, in part, in endowing the region with several carousels that run throughout the summer for children in local parks to enjoy. The story goes that, as a child, Johnson didn't have enough money to ride on a carousel, so, as an adult, he wanted to make sure no child in his cities faced the same thwarted desire. The carousels are anchors in each of the large parks throughout the Binghamton area, and from Memorial Day through Labor Day children can ride them for free. In "Walking

Distance," Young Marty Sloan is also riding a carousel when his older, time-traveling version tries to confront him. The older version finds himself with a car in need of an oil change just a mile and a half from his hometown of Homewood (which doesn't exist, sadly). He walks into town and finds his way to the soda jerk he frequented as a child. Over a soda with three scoops of ice cream—still 10 cents, like when he was a boy—he reflects on his surprise at returning to Homewood to find it unchanged. He tells the soda jerk, "The town looks the same, too. Pretty amazing, you know. Twenty years to look so exactly the same. . . . I always thought if I ever came back here, everything would be all changed. You know, nothing recognizable. Instead, it's just as if I'd left yesterday." He spends much of the rest of the episode trying to talk to his younger self, if only to impress on him that these are "wonderful years," which stand apart from the drudgery he faces as a media executive in New York City, where he seems to live a well-fêted life. The suburban charm, the modest conveniences of Homewood call to him across the years—so uncomplicated, so appealing. But in his final attempt to talk to his younger self, staged on a whirling carousel, young Marty trips and injures his leg. Counseled by his younger father, Old Martin is told that we each "only have one summer," and that this summer should be left to young Marty. Mysteriously returned to the present, Old Martin now has a "bum leg," confirming that his time travel wasn't merely a psychotic break brought on by workplace stresses. In Old Martin's present, the soda shop is full of teenagers, the three-scoop soda has increased in price to 35 cents; time has moved on. Yet, Homewood seems not to have fundamentally changed. One major difference, however, is that the carousel is now broken, like Martin. There's no more spinning around to be had, whether the slightly pleasurable version of the carousel or the slightly painful version Martin's regrets propel him through, culminating in the actual time travel he experiences.

Sometimes I feel like I've been displaced in time, too. Not out of some adulthood malaise that conspires to make me feel like there was some lost opportunity in my bucolic childhood but in the sense that, temporally, Binghamton exists at some prior time compared to California. That might sound snobbish in its way, but I don't mean it in a general sense but a rather specific one: all of the anxieties about—and pleasures projected into—the future that Californians evidenced, about climate change, about looming ecological disasters, about ever-upward creeping home values and decreasing public support for social services, seem to be all but absent here. Like Old Martin's spin on the carousel, it feels like New Yorkers in the Southern Tier are stuck in a temporal loop—there's nothing to stop the carousel from spinning, no real threat on the horizon—or at least not a threat that one can reasonably predict. Instead, there's the unpredictable weirdness of the Plume and its seeping into people's homes and bodies, and the catastrophic surges of the Susquehanna River into floods.

First in 2006 and then again in 2011, Binghamton and its neighbors experienced floods that destroyed businesses and homes and flooded streets to the point of necessitating evacuation. You'd be forgiven for not knowing anything about it. Despite being declared an emergency in the state, it lacked the public spectacle that other floods benefited from, like President George W. Bush's mishandling of Hurricane Katrina in 2005 and the future-now climate-change Hurricane Sandy in 2012. In comparison, the floods in Binghamton affected very few people, and they caused much less financial loss. It wasn't the defining moment of a presidency, nor even that of the governor of New York. Its tragedies were local, and the repetition of the event has had a numbing effect. By the time we were looking at homes in the area, our realtor reassured us that flood insurance—provided by our local insurance agent and underwritten by the U.S. government for pennies on the dollar—would cover any losses we might incur. The woman selling us her home assured us that if the house flooded, she would give us our money back—it hadn't flooded in either the hundred-year flood of 2006 or five-hundred-year flood of 2011. What were the chances that it could flood in the future? It seemed like a safe bet. But we had encountered the same kind of catastrophe callousness in

California, particularly regarding earthquakes. For the most part, they're just a part of everyday life, made banal by their repetition. When true disaster strikes, the government is there to ensure that homeowners are reimbursed for their losses. What's to lose? My neighbor's joke as we shoveled snow indexed the same banality: mudslides and wildfires are something to really worry about; floods don't even merit notice. And, sure enough, when we have had floods, usually as a result of snow melting or heavy rains, the water level of the river rises gently, in entirely expected ways. It's fascinating to watch the river rise into our yard, flooding close to the river, then inching up toward the rise that leads up to our house. It reaches a peak and then slowly creeps back to the river, creating large puddles in the otherwise-ignorable recesses in our yard, which waterfowl take advantage of for a day or so. The floods also bring beavers up river, who set about dam building, which we watch with great interest. The floods come and they go—just a part of living here, a catastrophe that has been tamed by its banality. And by the state's ability to ensure that property value is maintained or replaced.

The overwhelming feeling here is that the future happens elsewhere. That's what I get from Serling's "Walking Distance." Time moves on in New York City, but in little Homewood, time spins in circles like the carousel. It might look like time moves on, but the soda shop is full of another crop of teenagers, just like Old Martin was once; the soda jerk is just another white guy, wearing the same uniform. The only things that seem to change are the economy and machinery, evident in the rising costs of sodas and the breakdown of old carousels. But, in Serling's hometown of Binghamton, the carousels keep spinning. Maybe that's because the future as it happens elsewhere is just terrifying, and in nearby New York City, the future doesn't seem far off at all.

Douglas Cheek's *C.H.U.D.* (1984) tells a simple, familiar story of New York City. As a result of the U.S. government burying nuclear waste under the streets of Manhattan, specifically SoHo, a race of cannibalistic mutants develops from the homeless people who are exposed to the radioactive material. The mutants live in the sewers, preying largely on the human homeless. Occasionally, they strike out into the surface world, coming up through manhole covers to capture unsuspecting prey. The mutants—who come to be called Chuds, which stands for Cannibalistic Humanoid Underground Dwellers—take the wife of a local police captain in this way and set into motion the plot of the film, which revolves around the police search for this missing woman and other surface dwellers that have gone missing. An inordinate amount of time is spent in meetings of old white men, as our police captain attempts to get to the bottom of the mystery of why the city government would prefer that he give up trying to find the increasing number of missing people. The conspiracy that Captain Bosch (yes, he seems to be named for Heironymus Bosch, that painter of hellscapes) uncovers is that the city government is in cahoots with the U.S. government and that what C.H.U.D. actually stands for is "Contamination Hazard Urban Disposal." The mutants are a byproduct of the government's attempt to hide the radioactive waste that experimental projects have created, and rather than admit the mistake, the government liaison, referred to only as Wilson, is prepared to flood with natural gas the underground tunnels where the Chuds live and set them alight, thereby burning away the evidence both of the radioactive disposal and the flesh-eating mutants. When confronted by Bosch—"Are you crazy? You'll blow up the whole city!"—Wilson coolly replies, "I'm not going to flood the whole city. Only a section of SoHo." In that interchange, the politics of the film are made clear: the homeless, poor, and bohemians who inhabit SoHo in the early 1980s, well before its gentrification, are worthless to the government. They aren't flesh-eating mutants, but they might as well be.

Alongside Captain Bosch's investigation, the film follows two other investigators: a reverend who runs a soup kitchen and has noticed that a number of his clients are missing and a photographer who is attempting to break into journalism by documenting the lives of homeless New Yorkers. The three narratives converge in the final moments of the film, as Bosch and Wilson confront one another above the tunnels of SoHo, where the reverend and photographer have uncovered the true meaning of C.H.U.D. As Bosch confronts Wilson aboveground, he explains, "I know what C.H.U.D. stands for. Cannibalistic, my ass! Contamination Hazard Urban Disposal. You're nothing but the government garbage man. You take industrial waste, you take toxic sludge from every research project, and you dump it right here under the streets of our city." The city is dangerous. Not just because of flesh-eating mutants, or radioactive dumping, or government neglect, but as the city itself, at the cusp of the future. As our photographer and his fiancée discuss their new pregnancy and how it will change their lives, the mother-to-be suggests they move into her father's old house, somewhere in the suburbs. She explains, "It's a nice house. Be a nice place for a kid growing up." To which the photographer plays his urbane part and responds, "Yeah, but it's in the suburbs." Nodding yes, she replies, "Safe. I hate to think of our kids growing up here. It's scary." This is before she finds a dead dog hung by its leash in their basement, apparently disposed of there by the Chuds. This is also before she finds herself trapped in the apartment she shares with the photographer, a Chud lurking in the hallway outside their door, waiting to eat her. The city is, by its very nature, "scary," and the suburbs are "safe." Their safety is predicated on their repetitive nature: they will move into her father's old home and raise a family, and the intergenerational social reproduction will continue. But, like with the Plume in Endicott, and the corporate and government neglect of the toxic dumping that occurred, there is always the possibility that the suburban idyll they seek will be disrupted. How it will be disrupted is impossible to know—the future is too unpredictable, too potentially catastrophic—but the figure of the mutant Chud captures this unpredictability perfectly.

The Nihilism of Deep Time:
Man after Man and After

I MUST HAVE BEEN 11 or 12 when I first encountered the work of Dougal Dixon, a Scottish paleontologist turned speculative fabulist. At the time, Dixon's *After Man* (1998) had inspired a touring exhibit of his models of animal life on Earth thousands and millions of years in the future. Life-sized dioramas had been installed in the Hands-On Museum in Ann Arbor, which my class visited on a field trip. The dioramas depicted animals set free to evolve in an environment after humanity's extinction, returned to a state where natural selection could reassert itself against the domestication efforts and environmental tinkering that has driven many species extinct. Dixon depicted a future that was simultaneously impossible to imagine (for me) and rendered in the flesh. For Dixon, however, the future cleared of human interference is easy to plot out—evolution, for him, is a game of imagining how species will respond to emergent environmental conditions, and having the time without human interference to allow nature to take its course. Step by step, animals that were once domesticated or pushed to the brink of extinction claw their way back to assert themselves in the postapocalyptic world they have inherited. But Dixon manages to tame mutation; he makes it so domestic and denuded. Mutation is so much more surprising when it actually happens because it defies easy prediction and thwarts theory.

It took me years to rediscover Dixon. I didn't purchase a copy of *After Man* at the time—I don't even know if I knew that it existed. Nor did I buy *Man after Man* (Dixon 1990) when it was published. Only through the internet and a string of now-forgotten search terms did I finally turn Dixon up, as well as his work. If

After Man was a speculative fantasy of life on Earth's resurgence after the Anthropocene, *Man after Man* is humanity's ultimate humiliation in the face of the world they had created. Reading it now, it's hard to disassociate Dixon's work from recent discussions of the Anthropocene because he shares a nihilism of deep time, a sense that, deep enough in the future, it doesn't really matter what happens to humans. That may be true, but it disables work in the present. And what's particularly destabilizing is Dixon's recourse to an understanding of human biology, of innate drives, being the motor in our debasement—a view that Elizabeth Kolbert echoes in her Pulitzer Prize–winning *The Sixth Extinction* (2014).

Quoting evolutionary geneticist Svante Pääbo, Kolbert writes,

> [*Homo erectus*] never came to Madagascar, never to Australia. Neither did Neanderthals. It's only fully modern humans who start this thing of venturing out on the ocean where you don't see land. Part of that is technology, of course; you have to have ships to do it. But there is also, I like to think or say, some madness there. You know? How many people must have sailed out and vanished on the Pacific before you found Easter Island? I mean, it's ridiculous. And why do you do that? Is it for the glory? For immortality? For curiosity? And now we go to Mars. We never stop. (Kolbert 2014, 251)

Pääbo is invested in unraveling the "madness gene" by comparing *Homo sapiens* DNA with our ancestors and cohabitants—is there something uniquely human, something in our very genes, that drives humans to strike out into the open sea not knowing whether there is land to be found? The same "madness gene" might be at the heart of all human technological—and social—development: where Neanderthals were seemingly content with a simple set of technologies that they used for what seems to be centuries (Wynn and Coolidge 2012), *Homo sapiens* constantly pushed the technological edge, developing stone blades, ceramics, then bronze working, and eventually iron working (Basalla 1989). Stone axes gave way to bronze spears, which gave way to iron swords. Rafts gave way to kayaks and canoes, which gave way to ships. Like Vonnegut's view of the human drive to tinker in *Player Piano*,

Pääbo sees something intrinsic to human nature that pushes us toward "madness," toward possible self-destruction in the face of exploration and technological development. The archaeological record of the Neanderthal is still developing, so conceptions of their technological and social developments will likely change over time, but so too should our understandings of what drives humans to make the decisions they do. Was the madness of exploration spurred by sheer, genetic curiosity, or was it spurred by a lack of food and resources? The difference is meaningful for how we interpret the variations between *Homo sapiens* and their predecessors and cohabitants but also for how we think about ways out of our current situation. Is catastrophe inevitable, is it bred into us, or is it something that we choose? If catastrophe is inevitable, then nihilism is the corollary; if catastrophe is a choice, then we can choose otherwise.

Recounting a trip into the Grotte des Combarelles, in which she has to crawl, carrying artificial light so as to be able to see the paintings on the cavern's walls, Kolbert reflects on what the experience must have been like historically for our ancestors. She writes, "[The] ceiling was so low that the only way to move through the cave would have been to crawl, and the only way to see in the absolute blackness would have been to carry fire. Something—perhaps creativity, perhaps spirituality, perhaps 'madness'—drove people along nonetheless" (Kolbert 2014, 257). For Kolbert, there's something particularly human about the combination of "creativity," "spirituality," and "madness." The impulse for some prehistoric person to foray into a dark cave, paints and fire in hand, is indissociable from the drives that humans have toward the kinds of technological developments that have made the Anthropocene so devastating for life on Earth. Another dominant species—say the seemingly placid and technologically incurious Neanderthals—would have led to a different era, a different world order that might be more inclined toward environmental stewardship rather than extractive, capitalist resource monopolies and entrenched social inequalities (see Sawyer 2002). But, alas, in these biologically reductive theories of human nature, that is not the species we are—or, at least, conceptualizing humans as inherently driven toward particular kinds of self-destructive acts enables a form of deep-time nihilism, historically, presently, and in the future. Self-destruction is the price we pay for all of the great things we enjoy, from art and cultural expressions, to science and technology, to the social forms we are invested in, from the family to governments. Self-destruction is inevitable, and if there is any hope for humanity to survive, it can only be in a significantly altered form.

Enter Dixon and the speculative fabulation of *Man after Man*. Writing in 1990, Dixon sees the end of humanity approaching and, like Kolbert, sees it as an effect of the Anthropocene. Whether through climate change or nuclear holocaust, humanity will irrevocably alter our environment to the point where we will no longer be adapted to it. For Dixon, the primary motor in human development, both biologically and socially, is natural selection. Over the millennia that first led to the development of life on Earth and then the speciation that led to modern humans, humans developed to exquisitely fit our environments, from the air we breathe to the foods we eat. The irony of the Anthropocene is that the environment will no longer support us due to the creeping mismatch between what humans have evolved to do and the world that we have created as a by-product of our drive to madness. Given the dangers of the Anthropocene, and the compressed time scale on which we have to operate in the effort to develop a solution, if not for ourselves, then for life on Earth more generally, the answer that Dixon strikes on is to engineer our successors. First come the vacuum-friendly *Homo caelestis*, engineered to aid in the launching of generation ships for selected modern humans to escape into the depths of space in search of other homes. With that task done, the sterile Vacuumorphs are left to die out. Meanwhile, on Earth, bioengineering leads to a variety of experiments: water-borne *Homo aquaticus*, forest-dwelling *Homo silvis*, the plains-dwelling *Homo campis*, woodland-dwelling *Homo virgultis*, and the tundra-dwelling *Homo glacis*. The humans that are left pursue two routes, with some, after civilization's total collapse, adopting a new pastoralism and living off the land in a sustainable way until their eventual extinction. The lack of technology leaves them unable to deal with epidemic disease, further environmental change, and, eventually, the shift in the magnetic poles, which removes the electromagnetic protection from solar rays and leads to widespread cancers and birth defects. The other humans left adopt a cybernetic lifestyle, grafting themselves into prosthetic machines that support them, regardless of changes in environment; synthetic organs sustain life regardless of foodstuff or atmospheric conditions. But the mechanical humans obscure natural selection with their reliance on prosthetics, and, over time, they breed themselves into decrepitude and infertility. They, too, are left to their engineered extinction. The fabricated species who have been made, however, are left to adapt to the changing environment, having been given the capacities needed for the new world they live in—a world in which the Anthropocene has ended, nature is reasserting itself, and there is time enough for natural selection to take control once more.

Man after Man is a narrative encyclopedia. Broken up by time period—200 hundred years hence, then 500, 1000, 2000, 5000, 10,000, 50,000, 500,000, then 1, 2, 3, 5 million years into the future—Dixon doesn't follow characters, but species. He is interested in what happens to these human-like species, given time. But first he needs to allow the humans who are left to die off, and a recurrent behavior among the technologically dependent and pastoral humans is a resigned suicide. Greerath, a young prosthetically supported worker, provides a view of this impulse toward death in recounting the retirements of two friends:

> No matter how degenerate a human body became there were always the technological systems to keep it alive.
> The result was certainly a triumph over the raw wildness of nature, but there *must* be a better way. Machines keep breaking down and the food and drug supplies are constantly disrupted. Synthetic organs must hold the key.

> If they improve, muses Greerath, that would put her and many like her out of work. . . . That might not be a bad thing. She would like to devote more of her time to listening to music, looking at art, and wallowing in the newly-developing medium of hypnotic-involvement drama.
>
> Then, with a start, she remembers two friends who recently retired from work to do just that—and both of them switched off their life-supporters after a few days. Probably their stimulant-mix was wrong. (Dixon 1990, 34–35)

At once, Greerath is alien and familiar. Her life, like that of her reader, is sustained by deliberate mastery of the natural world, albeit in her case it is taken to the point of grotesque parody, her body suspended in a metal carriage that holds her external organs, each made to facilitate her ability to live in the ever-changing world. Greerath and her kin are our cybernetic present extrapolated to their flesh-horror ends: where we depend on vehicles for mobility, industrially produced food, municipally filtered water, pharmaceuticals for fighting disease, televisions and computers for entertainment and communication, Greerath and her fellow *machinadiumentum* have miniaturized these technologies and grafted them into themselves; they have become their machines. Our machinic successors pump chemicals directly into their biological systems, maintaining their mood pharmaceutically; they eat vat-grown foodstuff. But, like us, they work and seem to find social meaning in that labor; they too can't seem to imagine what life would be like without the disciplinary regimentation of the workplace, and, when left to admire art, listen to music, and enjoy "hypnotic-involvement drama," they seem to recognize the futility of a life lived without work. The anticapitalist revolution seems to have been delayed in the face of environmental degradation and the effects of climate change. Years later, when the magnetic poles shift, the prescient Durian Skeel understands the danger he and the other posthumans face. Rather than face the changes afoot, Skeel "is not waiting. Purposefully and methodically he disconnects each of his life-support devices and lapses into peaceful oblivion" (Dixon 1990, 54). Skeel, like Greerath's disillusioned, apathetic retiree friends, offer one choice: self-annihilation. That, it seems, is a reasonable decision to make, facing a future in which one's species faces little to no prospects of continuance—at least not in their current form. What underlies such an act is not just a will to negation, but a species resignation, as if the future has no value if one's species isn't there to dominate it. The Anthropocene may be a travesty, but for Kolbert, Päärt, and Dixon it's our travesty—it is an outgrowth of human will to dominate the natural environment, of our "madness gene."

That will to self-annihilation stands in juxtaposition to a trans-species empathy that Dixon's creatures exhibit periodically. As if their shared ancestral stock has bred into them a sense of common humanity across their physiological and behavioral differences, these successors sometimes see past their immediate needs—eating, mating, protecting themselves and kin—to a shared project, even if it is one that exceeds them as individuals. While hunting, Rumm, a forest-dweller some thousands of years hence, stumbles on a pack of roving tundra-dwellers. Seeing the opportunity to feed himself and his family, he decides to prey upon the strange creatures, despite the features they share with him.

> Silently he pounces upon [a young tundra-dweller's] back and the youngster stiffens beneath him and gives out a single, high-pitched plaintive yell, like one of his own babies crying.
> That yell almost stops the attack, so human is it; but he presses home his advantage. Throwing his hand over the creature's broad nose and mouth, stifling the unnerving noise, he wrenches its head backwards, into the folds of its neck. A cracking noise tells Rumm that the move has been satisfactorily fatal, and the body goes limp. (Dixon 1990, 56)

Dixon suggests that humanity is more than skin-deep, and that lesson motivates the humans who engineer their successors in the first place: if they can't inhabit the Earth, then some humans will, even if they are barely recognizable as such. The project of making this varied pack of posthumans is to extend the Anthropocene—albeit in different terms. Rumm and his fellows live in harmony with nature. They are driven by the pure, self- and community-directed compulsion to meet basic needs of food and biological reproduction; anything more than that, they seem to instinctively know, would only lead them down the path to destruction again. Yet, those drives are species-centric, and despite Rumm's inkling that there is something shared between him and his prey, that is insufficient to stop him from his violence. Shared humanity loses to species-needs. Or, maybe, it would be better to think of these needs as racial, as justified by an assumption of insurmountable difference between Rumm and his prey.

Dixon also imagines something akin to the "madness gene" motivating human action and underlying the Anthropocene. Our engineered successors seem to be burdened by the same biological compulsion, yet their drives to self-sustenance and species continuance short circuits the tinkering impulse that might lead to more technological solutions to the challenges they face. As a water-borne *aquaticus* reflects, something must hold back the impulse to innovate for fear that the old Anthropocene will reassert itself, dooming his world of posthumans to their own self-made apocalypse, one that they similarly won't have the time to adapt to:

> Ghloob peers through the watery film and the gelatinous envelope over his eyes. . . . but the days of easy and pleasant life disappeared long before his birth. It is said that once the sea, their home, supplied all their needs, but then their numbers became too many, and all the food was gone. Famine raged. Whole populations perished and sank into the dark deeps. Sometimes after famine, the fish, krill and plankton would return, but this food source was never enough. As soon as it came back it was exploited and destroyed once more. Nothing can be done about it: if they want to survive, they have to eat; if they eat they lose what they have and die. . . . Is there nothing they can do to feed their people without making things worse and worse and worse, and destroying all that they have? (Dixon 1990, 90, 93)

Poor Ghloob watches one of his friends get brutally murdered while they venture on land in search of food—the aquatics have become prey for their cousins, the woodland-dwellers, who lie in wait above the vegetation line, and move much faster than their water-based relatives. And they seem to feel no compunction about murdering their cousins, so far are they both removed from a common humanity. On one hand, Ghloob sees the dangers that he and his community face as they live hand-to-mouth: they're driven to exploit natural resources as they are provided them, sure to spend all their gained boon on reproduction, leading to an inevitable crash in resources, famine, and, potentially, the end of the species. But on the other hand, individuals and, sometimes, whole groups are lost to the dangers they face on land as they forage for food. They have been engineered to favor their species continuance over their individual needs; the "madness gene" seems to have been suppressed, and in so doing individuals willingly put themselves at risk. The will to self-annihilation is contained in support of species continuance.

Dixon posits that "loss" is what operates to inhibit the "madness gene." Among his many posthuman creatures there arise those he refers to as "memory people," individuals who are able to tap into inherited memories that stretch back generations in their origins (see Sheldrake 2009). These memory people are able to find resources—water, food—that are otherwise unapparent to their kin thanks to a preternatural knowledge that has been genetically handed down to them. Whether this is engineered into them or a result of natural selection is unclear, but it is based in their biology—there is no transmitted "culture" or knowledge that they are able to access. These memories motivate action and they help individuals keep themselves and their species alive through the procurement of resources, but they also seem to ensure that the "madness gene" is held in check. Among the otherwise complacent posthumans arise a group of "boatbuilders," individuals who begin to experiment with ironworking and shipbuilding after generations of these technologies being unexplored:

> They know, deep inside them, that the knowledge their ancestors gained, generation by generation, eventually destroyed them. They

know that their ancestors made things, that they took power from the sun and the sea, from the ancient concentrated remains of life, from the breakdown of the very forces that held matter together . . . Eventually the Earth became too crowded and burdened to carry them, and they perished under the weight of their own technical cleverness. All this they remembered, although they hardly understood it; but the inherited memory of the loss of everything that their ancestors had achieved was enough to forbid the use of inherited memory and the means of achieving it. (Dixon 1990, 86)

The boatbuilders are driven from their community. Fanatics who see their tinkering ways as endangering the species force them to flee from the island upon which they live. Their pursuers are not so orthodox that they won't use the tools left behind by the boatbuilders to hunt and exterminate them, so strong is the feeling of loss that motivates the suppression of the "madness gene." But loss is not enough, and when loss proves insufficient, murder ensures that the species will continue past the tinkering of a select few innovators.

Elsewhere, Dixon describes "strength" as the means through which these inherited memories and the will to tinker are held in check. Due to the dearth of natural resources, over time the plains-dwelling herbivores that have been engineered begin to develop a rudimentary society akin to insect hives. One female is chosen to breed to ensure that the population remains low enough to be supported by the available resources, and the rest of the community is organized to support her and the children that she bears in their communal hive. Males are sent off as hunters and food gatherers, and females are left in the hive to support the mother and her children. In considering how society might be innovated, Dixon narrates the value of this "strength":

It is a sign of their strength that they know how to make their life easier, but ignore the knowledge. Any one of them has enough inherited knowledge to dig the burning stones or the naturally-distilled organic fluid from the ground . . . and use their heat to melt down metal minerals. They could all break down the substances from the rocks and use them for many varied purposes. They know it is possible to fly to the moon and stars, and they know how to do it; but they will not. They will not call down the destruction once more. (Dixon 1990, 94)

"Strength," transspecies empathy, "loss," boatbuilding and the will to tinker, species continuance, reproduction, and subsistence. These seem to be the drivers in human existence so far as Dixon is concerned. He imagines our successors as our betters, more able to suppress the "madness gene" in favor of species continuance. This comes into relief 5 million years in the future, when humans have come to resemble anteaters, sabertooth tigers, and enormous sloths. They live, Dixon tells us, in balance with nature, all hereditary memories long since lost, all desires to tinker also weeded out through natural selection. There will never be another Anthropocene, at least not at the hands of these posthumans. But then those humans who left 5 million years in the past to seed other planets return, and they come back as aliens, adapted to environments they found to be their new homes. They seem not to have learned the lesson of the Anthropocene and return to Earth to mine it of its resources, living and not. Over time, these little alien *Homo* alter and corrupt the environment, initiating humanity's final humiliation: all of those strange, engineered posthumans are treated as nothing more than food and pack animals for the aliens, and when their utility comes to an end, so does the alien colonization of Earth. They move on, unromantically, to the next planet to harvest, to another Anthropocene to be set into motion, remorselessly, to support the species through its next colonization effort.

The nihilism of deep time—whether it comes in the form of thinking that humans have some kind of "madness gene" or that regardless of what we do to learn from our mistakes, we are doomed to repeat them—supports a damned-if-we-do, damned-if-we-don't approach to the Anthropocene and catastrophes in general. If the apocalypse is written into our very genetic code, if it is what makes us distinctly human—both in relation to our predecessors but also our imaginary successors—then the best we can do is make the most of an inevitable situation. There are two things that I find disagreeable with such a position: that humans are determined first and foremost by our biologies, and that time can only be conceived as a linear, progressive force. In terms of the former, centuries of philosophical and social scientific research has attempted to differentiate humans from our animal kingdom relatives, to find something truly distinctive about us that would explain our uniqueness—why there can be the Anthropocene but hasn't been an Insectocene or Beavercene. The reasoning of biological reductionists—which Dixon and Pääbo seem to be—is that human distinctiveness must be evident in our bodies, in our biologies, and that whatever worldly products humans might make that stand apart from what termites or beavers might produce are merely outgrowths of our biological programming, our will to tinker. In such a conception, what they miss is that influence is the process of slow accrual. The Anthropocene wasn't made in a day but was assembled through a diversity of forces, many of which were compelled by capitalist greed that found building momentum in the industrialization of labor. What seems like biological desire or species inevitability has been built over time through a variety of forces that have made us the modern subjects that we are; if we are invested in the Anthropocene as our humiliation, it is because of the subjects that we have been made to be. But it could be otherwise. Progressive time is a story that those in power employ to render their position inevitable: the way that things are is the inevitable effect of a set of processes that has produced this hegemony of the North Atlantic, of white people, of the elite. It couldn't be otherwise, so the thinking goes. But that's not true either. History is suffused with contingency, and history lingers. For progressivists, time passes, but counterontologies posit that time works differently, that it is recursive and haunting. And in that recursivity, there might be another way forward, another way to think about inevitability and what can be done with the influences and forces that have brought us to this pre-apocalyptic moment.

Mutating Temporalities: Slipstream Christopher Columbus

DOBY SAXON IS A TEENAGER living on the Blackfeet reservation in Montana. Doby is a little troubled, having been raised by an absentee father and overstressed mother; his family is poor, and they live in a rural setting near Glacier National Park, far removed from any urban center. They live a simulacrum life, something like what their ancestors lived—hunting elk, with permits provided by the state—but with the influences of settler colonialism. Now they have casinos, markets, automobiles, schools. Doby, like many of his peers, struggles with daily life on the reservation, but Doby seems especially tortured, and the cause is unclear. Things escalate to the point where he attempts suicide, standing in the freeway in an attempt to be struck by an unsuspecting driver. Meanwhile, a century beforehand, Francis Dalimpere is assigned as the government agent to the Blackfeet. He has a difficult time communicating with the chief of the tribe, Yellow Tail, and slowly becomes unstable, writing ever more oblique and fevered letters to the fiancée he is separated from. Things culminate in the nineteenth century when Francis is tasked with distributing a winter's rations to the tribe and accidentally ends up spoiling the meat the tribe needs to survive the winter—all in a disciplinary attempt to punish the tribe for seeming transgressions against his authority. The tribe faces famine, and Francis is wracked with guilt for his behavior. The suggestion is that the future of the Blackfeet is determined in this one moment, this one decision made by an unstable, disciplinary, white government agent. From that one event, their future is determined, leading to Doby's suicide attempt. And Doby's desire to kill himself seems

91

to be motivated by having found Francis's letters to his fiancée—and realizing that he is Francis reincarnated, doomed to live in the future that his decisions have created.

History haunts. That is the suggestion of Stephen Graham Jones's *Ledfeather* (2008), where the afterlife of colonial decisions is played out. And where white Americans are usually exempt from having to live with the consequences of the decisions made during the period of westward expansion—and maintained by practices today—Francis is burdened, seemingly forever, to be reincarnated on the reservation, living through the consequences again and again. The realizations might not always come—he might not find the letters written to his fiancée, he might not come to suspect the recursive nature of his experience—nevertheless he will be burdened to live the life his decisions wrought. But it may not be the case that time is operating in this cyclical way; instead, Francis and Doby might be in the "slipstream" of time, a conception of temporality and history that sees time as occurring simultaneously (Dillon 2012). Moments, persons, events, all exist in parallel. Causality is not linear so much as it is sympathetic. Francis's sins are revisited upon him forever, in parallel, an echo chamber of his own making. Slipstream collapses deep time. Rather than the nihilistic deferral that the displacement of the consequences of centuries of poor decision making allows, slipstream makes those consequences immediately present. The moral and ethical demands that deep time averts are unavoidable; all time, all history, is copresent, and the decisions that are made have immediate, if not always apparent, effects. Maybe this is why Francis unravels in the past, even before he has made the decision that will doom him. The fantasies of deep time—that we might be able to change something to save humanity, if not ourselves—are revealed as a progressivist delusion: there is no time other than the immediate moment, the immanent frame of now, and actions will be judged accordingly. As an indigenous writer, Jones uses slipstream as a mechanism to critique the progressive conception of time as a colonial artifact; for those living on the reservation, time doesn't proceed in the same way. Changing time, and changing history, depends on changing how people behave in the present, not in some backward-focused way but in the immanent moment.

At the heart of much speculative fiction about time are two questions: What if you could go back in time and change just one thing? What if one change could singlehandedly eradicate centuries of pain and death? No genocide in the Americas, no Atlantic slave trade, no environmental degradation as a result of unregulated industrialization; instead, the Americas will gently develop into a single empire able to peacefully ward off colonization, made possible by a syncretic approach to Christianity that allows the fusing together of European Christian traditions and indigenous religious cosmologies in the Americas. You'll be plucked from time to complete your mission, and all of your friends and family—your whole world and its history—will be wiped out as if they never occurred. Except that they did—they made you, after all, and you know how history was supposed to occur, and you'll have the records to prove it to those you meet in the past, just to ensure that history doesn't unfold like it did last time. This is the central conceit of Orson Scott Card's *Pastwatch: The Redemption of Christopher Columbus* (1997), a bureaucratic time-travel novel that posits that Christopher Columbus's visit to the Americas is the moment at which history tumbles into its progression toward the downfall of society and, eventually, the virtual extinction of the human species. The Anthropocene could have unfolded differently—it could have been a deliberate stewardship of peoples and the environment—if only Columbus's "discovery" of the Americas could have played out in a more coeval way. Tinkering with time to produce this mutant historiography becomes the moral demand of Card's Pastwatch future, as humanity will come to a virtual end otherwise. To ensure the future, a new past needs to be made.

Progressive time is at the heart of Card's mutant historiography. As Card explains,

No, explained the physicists, you're confusing causality with time. Time itself, as a phenomenon, is utterly linear and unidirectional.

Each moment happens only once, and passes into the next moment. Our memories grasp this one-way flow of time, and in our minds we link it with causality. We know that if A causes B, then A must come *before* B. But there is nothing in the physics of time that requires this. . . . Causality can be recursive, but time cannot. . . . Causality is irrational. (Card 1997, 215–17)

Card's physicists and mathematicians come to this conclusion by reckoning with the fact that another group of time travelers had already intervened in history to produce their (and, presumably, our) future. Those time travelers and their history can be said to exist insofar as they have had an impact on actual history, but as soon as they made those changes in history, their history ceased to exist. As Diko, one of the protagonists of the novel, explains, "Anything sent back in time is lifted out of the causal flow. It can no longer be affected by anything that happens to the timestream that originally brought it into existence, and when it enters the timestream at a different point, it becomes an uncaused causer. When we change the past, this present will disappear" (Card 1997, 201). They could make history, but would have no history of their own. This is possible, in Card's physics, because time is singular. In its progression, there are a series of moments, like stones in a path. There is only room for one stone for each step, and replacing a stone means that the prior stone no longer exists, but the actions that led to the movement of the stone do exist. The history that Pastwatch exists within has happened, until the moment in which they begin to undo it. In that moment, that history is extinguished from time, its stones removed from the path to make way for the unfurling of a new history. As the lead mathematician in charge of reckoning with the metaphysics of time travel explains, "the end will be painless. There will be no cataclysm. There will be no sense of loss. There will be no regret. Instead, there will be a new Earth. A new future" (Card 1997, 231). The choice to tinker with the past in this way is motivated by Card's characters' focus on cataloging human history with their Pastwatch technology, which first only allows them to observe the past, but eventually is refined to enable individuals to make one-way trips back in time. The history they observe is our history, full of pain and violence, full of neglect and abuse. The future that they face is one of immanent collapse: arable land is disappearing as a result of global warming and poor agricultural practices, populations around the world are confronting famine, and cheap, easily accessible fuel is no longer available. When civilization collapses, it will fall for good. If humanity survives the coming wars, famines, and epidemics, there will be no easy return to comfort. Instead, a new Stone Age will persist indefinitely. The pain, violence, and humiliations of this future can only be prevented through an intervention in the past.

This progressive view of time is explicitly put into conversation with a cyclical conception of time that Card ascribes to the indigenous people in the Americas. As Putukam, a seer among the people of Ankuash, explains, "I always thought that time moved in great circles, as if all of us had been woven into the same great basket of life, each generation another ring around the rim. . . . But when in the great circles of time was there ever such horror as these white monsters from the sea? So the basket is torn, and time is broken, and all the world spills out of the basket into the dirt" (Card 1997, 34). It's no mistake that Card puts this view of cyclical time into the mouth of an indigenous woman. As a romantic notion of cyclical time that stands in tension with the progressive time articulated by male scientists, it's marked as doubly irrational, associated with a woman and indigenous people; but for Card and his scientists, there is no return, no karmic wheel that spins, reincarnating individuals in a repetitive framework that persists as if without history. Time is linear and there is only one real history. The consequences of the decisions we make—and that our ancestors made—are ours to bear in a game of intergenerational hot potato. This indigenous way of reckoning time and history is literally displaced by the time travelers who return to the fifteenth century to right Columbus's wrongs—and, by extension, all of white Europe's. There is only one real history because there must be: if time were cyclical or if it were divergent, offering multiple possible timelines, the moral stakes of intervention would be nullified. Moreover, history isn't inevitable as a cyclical understanding of time and history would seem to posit; instead it must be malleable so as to make an intervention even possible. Yet, alongside this malleability there must be some forces that compel human action, that make history.

Rather than see the future as inevitably produced by some biological driver in human beings—the will to tinker, the self-destructive embrace of capitalism—Card sees history as contingent, as malleable, as something that can mutate if only exposed to the right forces. Card's temporal intervention is predicated on the malleability of history and the ability to install social norms that override "human nature." The inevitability of history—so far as it is inevitable—is an outcome of human desires that are self-destructive at their root. If the forces that shape human action can be changed, then history can be changed as well. As Hassan, one of Card's Pastwatch protagonists, explains, human history has finally resulted in a level of comfort and care that had previously eluded most societies—albeit only by sometime in the twenty-fourth century. Before knowing of the catastrophes that imminently face humanity, Hassan argues against the temporal intervention for precisely these reasons, suggesting that "Humanity is finally at peace. There are no plagues. No children die hungry or live untaught. The world is healing. That was not inevitable. It might have ended up far worse. . . . Do you imagine that there's some change we could make that would improve human nature? Undo the rivalry of nations? Teaching people sharing is better than greed?" (Card 1997, 46). "Human nature," nationalism, and "greed" are combined here to index those base human desires that caused so much seemingly inevitable harm throughout history. For Hassan, changing history might not affect these underlying drives, and events would play out as they had previously—a minor change in history might not be enough to change its arc. Had Columbus not arrived in the Americas, then someone else would, and history would unfold in the same, linear fashion, with the same apocalyptic results.

But underlying Card's speculative argument is his conception that Columbus is a "great man," a truly singular individual, able by himself to shape the actions of others. Columbus's ability to sway the queen and king of Spain to fund his exploration of the Atlantic Ocean in search of a path to China is exemplary of his abilities both to be able to see what others cannot and to be persuasive—both of which Columbus attributes to divine grace, but which Card sees as his immutable nature. Despite his greatness, Kemal, one of the historians involved in the intervention, argues that what Columbus uses his greatness for is contingent:

> There was nothing inevitable about [Columbus's] westward voyage at the time he sailed. The Portuguese were on the verge of finding a new route to the Orient. No one imagined an unknown continent. The wisest ones knew that the world was large, and believed that an ocean twice the width of the Pacific stretched between Spain and China. Not until they had a sailing vessel they believed was capable of crossing such an ocean would they sail west. . . . It was because Columbus came to America, with his relentless faith that he had found the Orient. Merely stumbling on the landmass meant nothing—the Norse did it, and where did that lead? . . . It was not the fact that *somebody* sailed west that led to the European conquest of America and thus the world. It was because *Columbus* did it. (Card 1997, 47)

Columbus is posited as a great man of history, an individual who can compel the actions of others, singlehandedly shaping history's course. Key to Columbus's greatness is his faith in a Christian god. The ability of the first Interveners to shape Columbus's actions depended on his piousness, convincing him that there was a New World to explore—and to convert to Christianity. Card sees Columbus's Christianity as malleable, too: when confronted with his racism by Diko, who has taken on the visage of Sees-In-The-Dark, a seer in Ankuash, he is quick to change his behaviors toward those he meets in the Americas, and to condemn the actions of his crew who continue to act in un-Christian fashion, even if such racism was practiced in fifteenth-century Europe without contradicting interpretations of Christianity. Columbus's Christianity is also supple enough to be shaped in such a way as to help engineer a move away from slavery. In so doing, the members of Pastwatch seek to minimize the pain and violence of our history, and to set social norms onto a more egalitarian path.

Among the discoveries that Pastwatch has overseen through their time-observation technology is that of Atlantis, a protocity in the plains that would become the Red Sea. Kemal, a Muslim historian, is the one who makes the discovery, and along with his observations of the mythical city, now proven to be real, he also learns that the Biblical Noah was also real—and the story of the flood that Noah foretells is both an environmental parable, and the beginning of a set of cultural practices that are adopted among the young civilizations that follow in Atlantis's wake. One of these practices is slavery, and as Kemal explains, it was the invention of one person:

> Slavery was not inevitable. It was invented, at a specific time and place. We know when and where the first person was turned into property. It happened in Atlantis, when a woman had the idea of putting the sacrificial captives to work, and then, when her most valued captive was going to be sacrificed, she paid her tribal elder to remove him permanently from the pool of victims. . . . It became the foundation of their city, the fact that the slaves were doing the citizens' duty in digging the canals and planting and tending the crops. Slavery was the reason they could afford the leisure to develop a recognizable civilization. . . . Slavery was a direct replacement for human sacrifice. (Card 1997, 94–95)

The practice of slavery and its malleability is set against the inevitable forces of human nature, and, here, Card sees slavery as based on "value." The first slave owner depends on the use of money, of a system of abstract value, which is able to substitute a cost for human life. From that initial purchasing of a human life, the European system of slavery slowly develops until it reaches the Americas and is fueled by the European expansion into Africa as well. Card compares that system of slavery, which depends on the abstractions of capitalism, to the forms of slavery that developed independently in the Americas. There, slavery remains steadfastly in support of sacrificial practices, never making the leap to the abstraction of life's value. It is no better, really, but doesn't propel the market system in the same way—and, as Card's indigenous American historian, Hunahpu, explains, it was about to lead to the downfall of the Aztecs: they simply couldn't produce enough food to feed their citizens as they sacrificed too many viable laborers. A reformed Columbus would be able to steer their practices away from sacrifice—and away from slavery altogether—through a syncretic understanding of Christ's sacrifice as the ultimate appeasement of the blood-hungry gods of Xibalba. It's hard here to separate Card's time-traveling tinkering with his own Mormonism, but it may be his own piousness that allows him to think beyond the seemingly inevitable forces of European Christianity and to embrace the promise of an American syncretism that could allow for an acceptance of doctrine that moved beyond orthodoxies and inquisitions. The future, Card suggests, must be syncretic; it might also need to be Christian. But if it is, it will be a mutant Christianity that allows for a diverse set of interpretations and practices. This might be unappealing for secularists, but Card suggests that the pragmatic use of Christianity might serve both as an antiracist ideology as well as the basis for a politics of environmental stewardship that averts the Anthropogenic apocalypse. Columbus is our Noah, and the linear history he will set in motion—in our time—is not the best possible series of events, but failing the invention of time-travel technologies, they are the series of events we are burdened to live through over and over in the slipstream of the Anthropocene.

Card's intervention in time points to the critical need for syncretism, the need to combine ways of thinking to move beyond the dogmatic theoretical positions defined by earlier modes of thought. Card wants to pervert readings of Christianity that are exclusionary and that motivate bigotry and violence. He also wants to create a challenge for contemporary readers to rethink their relationship to time, causality, and history. Taken together, Card's concerns ask readers to reassess their ethical frame for the present moment. If this is the timeline that results in an intervention that will eradicate it, is there something that can be done in the present to alter our timeline, without time travel? Jones does the same: in his recursive slipstream narrative that unsettles the decision making of colonial administrators in the past by forcing at least one of them to bear the consequences now in a constantly reverberating echo of time, causality, and history, can something be done to change the course of history? Those speculative questions are at once deeply theoretical—what is the nature of time, causality, and history?—and also deeply social. Social theory in this speculative idiom is not just a game of "what if?" but a challenge to complacency and resignation. Not content to simply diagnose the problem that faces society, speculative fiction asks us to think about how it might be otherwise and what might be done to bring a better future into being. Moving beyond staid efforts at diagnosis, social theory produced about what might be is necessarily unsettling. Card asks readers to consider whether they want history as they have known it to be eradicated as a result of their inaction. Jones asks readers if there is anything to be done in the present to change the course of history. They both ask, implicitly, whether we can mutate away the "madness gene" and its consequences to produce a better present and future. This mutation will be surprising and challenging and might not be something that anyone is ready for. But we know the present, with its inequities, violence, and fear. And we know the likely futures we face, even if we can't imagine their collective consequences. The blindnesses and comforts of the present contrive to obscure our likely futures.

There must be a way out.

Acknowledgments

Over coffee one morning, my partner Katherine suggested that I "write something about the future," after years of humoring my affection for sometimes questionable media. Our conversations continue, and I thank her for all of her support and encouragement. A few years previous, Jonathan Alexander and Rob Latham invited me to participate in a series of workshops on California and science fiction, which served as a spur for getting back to fiction, and I am grateful to them and other workshop participants for their spirited engagement. Most of all, I am grateful to Felix and Iggy for the future they'll bring into being through curiosity and cleverness.

Works Cited

Barthes, Roland. 1977. "The Death of the Author." In *Image—Music—Text*, translated by Stephen Heath, 142–48. New York: Noonday Press.

Basalla, George. 1989. *The Evolution of Technology*. New York: Cambridge University Press.

Behar, Ruth. 1996. *The Vulnerable Observer: Anthropology That Breaks Your Heart*. Boston: Beacon Press.

Bowler, Kate. 2013. *Blessed: A History of the American Prosperity Gospel*. New York: Oxford University Press.

Briggs, Charles L., and Mark Nichter. 2009. "Biocommunicability and the Biopolitics of Pandemic Threats." *Medical Anthropology* 28, no. 3: 189–98.

Brynjolfsson, Erik, and Andrew McAfee. 2014. *The Second Machine Age: Work, Progress, and Prosperity in a Time of Brilliant Technologies*. New York: W. W. Norton.

Butler, Octavia. 1993. *Parable of the Sower*. New York: Four Walls Eight Windows.

Butler, Octavia. 1997. *Dawn*. New York: Aspect.

Butler, Octavia. 1998. *Parable of the Talents*. New York: Seven Stories Press.

Card, Orson Scott. 1997. *Pastwatch: The Redemption of Christopher Columbus*. New York: Tor Books.

Cheek, Douglas. 1984. *C.H.U.D.* New World Pictures.

Clifford, James, and George Marcus, eds. 1986. *Writing Culture: The Poetics and Politics of Ethnography*. Berkeley: University of California Press.

Clinton, George, and Ben Greenman. 2014. *Brothas Be, Yo Like George, Ain't That Funkin' Kinda Hard On You? A Memoir*. New York: Atria Books.

Collins, Samuel. 2008. *All Tomorrow's Cultures: Anthropological Engagements with the Future*. New York: Berghahn.

Daston, Lorraine, and Peter Galison. 2007. *Objectivity*. New York: Zone Books.

Dekker, Fred. 1993. *Robocop 3*. Orion Pictures.

Desmond, Adrian, and James Moore. 1994. *Darwin: The Life of a Tortured Evolutionist*. New York: W. W. Norton.

Dick, Philip K. 2012a. *The Man in the High Castle*. New York: Mariner Books.

Dick, Philip K. 2012b. *Ubik*. New York: Mariner Books.

Dillon, Grace, ed. 2012. *Walking in the Clouds: An Anthology of Indigenous Science Fiction*. Tucson: University of Arizona Press.

Disch, Thomas. 1999. *334*. New York: Vintage.

Dixon, Dougal. 1990. *Man after Man: An Anthropology of the Future*. New York: St. Martin's Press.

Dixon, Dougal. 1998. *After Man: A Zoology of the Future*. New York: St. Martin's Press.

Eberhardt, Thom. 1984. *Night of the Comet*. Atlantic Releasing Corporation.

Edginton, Ian, and D'Israeli. 2003. *Scarlet Traces*. Milwaukie, Ore.: Dark Horse Comics.

Emmerich, Roland. 1996. *Independence Day*. 20th Century Fox.

Fanon, Franz. 2008. *Black Skin, White Masks*. Translated by Richard Philcox. New York: Grove Press.

Foucault, Michel. 1998. "What Is an Author?" In *Aesthetics, Method, and Epistemology*, edited by James D. Faubion, 205–22. Essential Works of Foucault 1954–1984. New York: New Press.

Gell, Alfred. 1998. *Art and Agency: An Anthropological Theory*. New York: Oxford University Press.

Gibson-Graham, J. K., Jenny Cameron, and Stephen Healy. 2013. *Take Back the Economy: An Ethical Guide for Transforming Our Communities*. Minneapolis: University of Minnesota Press.

Gordon, Avery. 1997. *Ghostly Matters: Haunting and the Sociological Imagination*. Minneapolis: University of Minnesota Press.

Haraway, Donna. 1997. *Modest_Witness@Second_Millennium. FemaleMan©_Meets_OncoMouseTM*. New York: Routledge.

Haraway, Donna. 2003. *The Companion Species Manifesto: Dogs, People, and Significant Otherness*. Chicago: Prickly Paradigm Press.

Haraway, Donna. 2008. *When Species Meet*. Minneapolis: University of Minnesota Press.

Hartigan, John. 1999. *Racial Situations: Class Predicaments of Whiteness in Detroit*. Princeton, N.J.: Princeton University Press.

Hartigan, John. 2014. *Aesop's Anthropology: A Multispecies Approach*. Minneapolis: University of Minnesota Press.

Harvey, David. 2005. *A Brief History of Neoliberalism*. New York: Oxford University Press.

Heckman, Davin. 2008. *A Small World: Smart Houses and the Dream of the Perfect Day*. Durham, N.C.: Duke University Press.

Heinlein, Robert. 1940. "If This Goes On—." *Astounding Science Fiction,* February.

Hymes, Dell, ed. 1974. *Reinventing Anthropology.* New York: Vintage Books.

Jones, Stephen Graham. 2008. *Ledfeather.* Tuscaloosa: University of Alabama Press.

Kershner, Irvin. 1990. *Robocop 2.* Orion Pictures.

Kirkman, Robert, and Charlie Adlard. 2015. *The Walking Dead.* Vol. 11. Portland, Ore.: Image Comics.

Kirksey, Eben, ed. 2015. *The Multispecies Salon.* Durham, N.C.: Duke University Press.

Klein, Naomi. 2007. *The Shock Doctrine: The Rise of Disaster Capitalism.* New York: Picador.

Kolbert, Elizabeth. 2014. *The Sixth Extinction: An Unnatural History.* New York: Henry Holt.

Lacey, Robert. 1986. *Ford: The Men and the Machine.* Boston, Mass.: Little, Brown and Company.

Lasch, Chistopher. 1979. *The Culture of Narcissism: American Life in an Age of Diminishing Expectations.* New York: W. W. Norton.

Latour, Bruno. 1987. *Science in Action: How to Follow Scientists and Engineers through Society.* Cambridge, Mass.: Harvard University Press.

Le Guin, Ursula K. 1969. *The Left Hand of Darkness.* New York: Berkley Publishing Group.

Le Guin, Ursula K. 1994. *The Dispossessed.* New York: HarperCollins.

Leonard, Elmore. 1977. *Unknown Man Number 89.* New York: Delacorte Press.

Lock, Margaret. 2002. *Twice Dead: Organ Transplants and the Reinvention of Death.* Berkeley: University of California Press.

Lutz, Catherine. 1995. "The Gender of Theory." In *Women Writing Culture,* edited by Ruth Behar and Deborah A. Gordon, 249–66. Berkeley: University of California Press.

Lutz, Catherine, and Anne Lutz Fernandez. 2010. *Carjacked: The Culture of the Automobile and Its Effect on Our Lives.* New York: St. Martin's Press.

Marx, Karl. 1992. *Early Writings.* Translated by Rodney Livingstone. New York: Penguin.

Marx, Karl, and Frederick Engels. 1998. *The Communist Manifesto: A Modern Edition.* New York: Verso.

Metzl, Jonathan M. 2003. *Prozac on the Couch: Prescribing Gender in the Era of Wonder Drugs.* Durham, N.C.: Duke University Press.

Morris, William. 1993. *News from Nowhere and Other Writings.* Edited by Clive Wilmer. New York: Penguin.

Robinson, Kim Stanley. 1984. *The Wild Shore.* New York: Tom Doherty Associates.

Robinson, Kim Stanley. 1988. *The Gold Coast*. New York: Tom Doherty Associates.

Robinson, Kim Stanley. 1990. *Pacific Edge*. New York: Tom Doherty Associates.

Rofel, Lisa. 1999. *Other Modernities: Gendered Yearnings in China after Socialism*. Berkeley: University of California Press.

Romero, George. 1978. *Dawn of the Dead*. United Film Distribution Company.

Romero, George. 2009. *Survival of the Dead*. E1 Entertainment Magnet Releasing.

Rose, Nikolas. 1996. *Inventing Our Selves: Psychology, Power, and Personhood*. New York: Cambridge University Press.

Sawyer, Robert. 2002. *Hominids*. New York: Tor Books.

Schrader, Paul. 1978. *Blue Collar*. Universal Pictures.

Shapin, Stephen, and Simon Schaffer. 1989. *Leviathan and the Air-Pump*. Princeton, N.J.: Princeton University Press.

Shaviro, Steven. 1993. *The Cinematic Body*. Minneapolis: University of Minnesota Press.

Shaviro, Steven. 2015. *Discognition*. London: Repeater Books.

Sheldrake, Rupert. 2009. *Morphic Resonance: The Nature of Formative Causation*. Rochester, Vt.: Park Street Press.

Soleri, Paolo. 1970. *Arcology: The City in the Image of Man*. Cambridge, Mass.: MIT Press.

Spinrad, Norman. 1972. *The Iron Dream*. New York: Avon Books.

Strathern, Marilyn. 1992. *Reproducing the Future: Anthropology, Kinship, and the New Reproductive Technologies*. New York: Routledge.

Sugrue, Thomas. 1998. *The Origins of the Urban Crisis: Race and Inequality in Postwar Detroit*. Princeton, N.J.: Princeton University Press.

Suvin, Darko. 1979. *Metamorposes of Science Fiction: On the Poetics and History of a Literary Genre*. New Haven, Conn.: Yale University Press.

Trouillot, Michel-Rolph. 2003. *Global Transformations: Anthropology and the Modern World*. New York: Palgrave Macmillan.

Turner, Frederick Jackson. 1998. *Rereading Frederick Jackson Turner: "The Significance of the Frontier in American History" and Other Essays*. New Haven, Conn.: Yale University Press.

Verhoeven, Paul. 1987. *Robocop*. Orion Pictures.

Vonnegut, Kurt. 2006. *Player Piano*. New York: The Dial Press.

Warren, Donald. 1996. *Radio Priest: Charles Coughlin, the Father of Hate Radio*. New York: Free Press.

Weheliye, Alexander. 2014. *Habeas Viscus: Racializing Assemblages, Biopolitics, and Black Feminist Theories of the Human*. Durham, N.C.: Duke University Press.

Wells, H. G. 2005. *The War of the Worlds*. New York: Penguin.

Wilson, Elizabeth A. 2004. *Psychosomatic: Feminism and the Neurological Body*. Durham, N.C.: Duke University Press.

Wolf, Eric R. 1982. *Europe and the People without History*. Berkeley: University of California Press.

Womack, Ytasha. 2013. *Afrofuturism: The World of Black Sci-Fi and Fantasy Culture*. Chicago: Chicago Review Press.

Wyndham, John. 1951. *The Day of the Triffids*. New York: Doubleday.

Wyndham, John. 2008. *The Midwich Cuckoos*. New York: Penguin.

Wynn, Thomas, and Frederick Coolidge. 2012. *How to Think Like a Neandertal*. New York: Oxford University Press.

X, Malcolm. 1970. *By Any Means Necessary*. New York: Pathfinder.

Yong, Ed. 2016. *I Contain Multitudes: The Microbes Within Us and a Grander View of Life*. New York: Ecco Press.

Young, Coleman, and Lonnie Wheeler. 1994. *Hard Stuff: The Autobiography of Coleman Young*. New York: Viking.

Youngquist, Paul. 2016. *A Pure Solar World: Sun Ra and the Birth of Afrofuturism*. Austin: University of Texas Press.

Matthew J. Wolf-Meyer is associate professor of anthropology at Binghamton University, State University of New York. He is author of *The Slumbering Masses: Sleep, Medicine, and Modern American Life* (Minnesota, 2012).